PIRATES
Adventurers of the High Seas

A heated battle between a squadron of Spanish warships and a host of Barbary corsairs. (National Maritime Museum, Greenwich)

PIRATES
Adventurers of the High Seas

DAVID F. MARLEY

ARMS AND
ARMOUR

Arms and Armour Press
An Imprint of the Cassell Group
Wellington House, 125 Strand, London WC2R 0BB

Distributed in the USA by Sterling Publishing Co. Inc.,
387 Park Avenue South, New York, NY 10016-8810.

Distributed in Australia by Capricorn Link (Australia) Pty. Ltd,
2/13 Carrington Road, Castle Hill, NSW 2154.

British Library Cataloguing-in-Publication Data:
a catalogue record for this book is available from the British Library

ISBN 1-85409-215-4

Flag artwork by Cilla Eurich
Cartography by Anthony A. Evans

Designed and edited by DAG Publications Ltd.
Designed by David Gibbons; layout by Anthony A. Evans;
edited by Michael Boxall;

Printed & bound in Slovenia by Printing House DELO-Tiskarna
by arrangement with Korotan Ljubljana

Contents

I

Cruel Seas

Sin their conception, their birth weeping:
Their life, a general mist of error,
Their death, a hideous storm of terror.
John Webster (*c.*1580–1638)

Since the dawn of time, the world's oceans have seen countless predators. Organised piracy flourished among the earliest civilisations of the Middle East, the coast of the Persian Gulf between Qatar and Oman being home to generations of sea-robbers, who plundered the shipping of the Assyrian kingdoms, and later harried the fleet of Alexander the Great. The warm, sparkling waters of the Mediterranean also bred many pirates, who in the last hundred years of the Roman Republic achieved such pre-eminence that they sacked four hundred towns along the Italian mainland, held a young Julius Caesar hostage for six weeks, and briefly checked the expansion of Roman rule itself. In China, similar activities dated from at least 400 AD, when the notorious San-Wen ravaged its northern seaboard and raised rebellion in the south.

Succeeding centuries were to witness a continual ebb and flow to piratical depredations, in every corner of the globe. The Cretans and Vikings took their turn in both southern and northern Europe, spreading fire and destruction over immense distances, while conquering remote new strongholds. Often the role of the truly successful pirate chieftain became that of seagoing mercenary as well, with monarchs seeking to buy his services through the granting of official commissions, in return for a share of booty.

One such case was the medieval rover known as Eustace the Monk, a fallen Flemish cleric allegedly having black magical powers, who plundered French shipping on behalf of England's King John in the early thirteenth century. When his greed led him to prey upon English ships as well, Eustace was forced to flee the realm in 1212, and sell his services to the rival French. A couple of years later this rover led an attempted invasion of England, his fleet being intercepted in the Straits of Dover. The English sailors blinded Eustace's crew by hurling lime at his flagship, followed by a deadly rain of arrows. His vessel was then boarded and the renegade Churchman decapitated on the spot.

With the dramatic expansion of sea traffic towards the end of the Late Middle Ages, however, the nature of piracy also began to change. Throughout the Dark Ages, voyages had been relatively infrequent, involving small tonnages and short distances, so that the interceptions or wreckings by crim-

Left: Sixteenth-century French rovers carrying booty aboard ship, while behind them a Caribbean town erupts in flames.

inals affected relatively few people. Indeed, many an impoverished coastal community felt completely justified in extorting tolls from ships passing through its waterways, or even robbing the occasional rich prize without the least pang of conscience. Such an attitude naturally allowed local predators to thrive.

But the far-reaching explorations of Italian, Portuguese and Spanish navigators during the latter half of the fifteenth century opened up a vast new dimension to sea travel, both in terms of its volume as well as its importance. Soon European merchant vessels were routinely sailing to distant Africa, Asia and America in search of exotic goods, which commanded such huge profits that the arrival of a single trading fleet might affect a whole nation's economy. Hence any interference with these voyages could have grave consequences, and central authorities began taking a dim view of piratical activities off their coasts.

However, while petty thuggery and brigandage might be easily subdued close to home, these far-flung new trade routes offered a tempting outlet for an entirely different breed of marauder, a mobile and elusive adventurer who could sail to the far ends of the earth, and seek his fortune amid its most lawless frontiers. Even legitimate merchantmen scarcely recognised any rules during this pioneering period, their vessels travelling well armed, and as ill-disposed towards competitors as they were towards their enemies. Furthermore, large national monopolies sought to maintain a tight, restrictive stranglehold over their overseas trade sources, to the point of fighting pitched battles with any rival, and even invoking the intervention of their home governments.

Thus many an honest trader might find himself labelled an interloper, or poacher, or even a pirate, merely for trespassing upon another nation's self-proclaimed preserve. Such hostility greeted the Plymouth merchant John Hawkins, when he made three voyages to Spanish America early in Queen Elizabeth I's reign. He departed on the first of these in 1562, pausing at Guinea in West Africa to load his three ships with three hundred black slaves, before traversing the Atlantic and selling these for a handsome profit to the plantation owners of Hispaniola, who welcomed him despite Madrid's prohibition against foreign vessels visiting its New World territories.

The profits from this first venture proved so lucrative that they made Hawkins the richest man in Plymouth, and attracted a host of investors for his second voyage, including the sovereign. After rounding up another four hundred African slaves, Hawkins arrived off the Spanish Main only to find its ports officially closed to him, in retaliation for his earlier Hispaniola venture. Nevertheless, through a combined show of force and friendly persuasion, he eventually managed to sell all his slaves and many other trade goods besides, arriving back in England in September 1564 with still greater wealth.

The Spanish Ambassador in London complained to the Queen, but Hawkins unabashedly assured her that his third crossing would be as peaceable as the first two, it being his intention merely 'to lade Negroes in Guinea and sell them in the West Indies in truck of gold, pearls and emeralds'. But after experiencing considerable difficulty in procuring slaves and disposing of them in the West Indies, Hawkins's six-ship flotilla was struck by a storm in the Gulf of Mexico in September 1568. Forced to seek refuge in Veracruz, he deceived the local Spaniards and seized their offshore island fortress of San Juan de Ulúa as a base in which to effect repairs.

The next day, however, the annual plate fleet arrived from Spain, trapping the Englishmen inside. Tense negotiations ensued to allow the Spanish merchant vessels to enter and the intruders to depart, climaxed midway by a surprise attack against the unprepared English ships. Only Hawkins's 300-ton vice-flagship *Minion* and the tiny 50-ton *Judith*, commanded by his 28-year-old kinsman Francis Drake, succeeded in cutting their way to freedom. Becoming separated, Drake's homeward passage proved uneventful, but Hawkins endured a nightmarish journey and arrived back in Plymouth with only fifteen crew-members still alive.

This battle of San Juan de Ulúa proved a watershed, so embittering relations between the two peoples that future English expeditions to the New World grew unmistakably more aggressive. Drake in particular sought to avenge Hawkins's defeat by a destructive rampage through the West Indies in 1572, high-

Above: Seventeenth century sea engagement

lighted by his capture of a rich mule train near Nombre de Dios, all in flagrant disregard of the official peace prevailing with Spain. Elizabeth publicly distanced herself from this campaign, but when Drake returned from a second, even more spectacular voyage in 1580 – having circumnavigated the globe and brazenly seized a wealthy Spanish galleon in the Pacific Ocean – she granted him an audience and questioned him for six hours regarding this epic cruise.

She then publicly bestowed a knighthood upon her paladin aboard *Golden Hind* at Deptford, amid great rejoicing and lavish ceremonies, and henceforth began referring to Drake affectionately as 'her pirate'. Such overt support, during a period of supposedly peaceful diplomatic relations with Spain, reinforced the outlaw appeal of any venture into the West Indies for the

English, while at the same time hardening Madrid's resistance to foreign encroachments upon its empire. By the time Drake departed on his third enterprise in 1585, war had exploded in the Low Countries, so that he commanded a full-blown naval expedition consisting of 21 warships and 2,300 soldiers, which launched massive strikes against both Cartagena and Santo Domingo.

The commencement of these hostilities provided ample employment for every sort of seagoing ruffian, in the form of privateering. Europe's royal navies were still extremely small establishments during the sixteenth century, only a few dozen men-of-war being owned outright by any government. Instead they granted commissions to private vessels during times of conflict, to conduct independent operations on their behalf, and in

return for spoils which had to be adjudicated before an Admiralty court. The resultant eighteen years of warfare until the close of Elizabeth's reign bred a new generation of rover, well schooled in prize-hunting upon the high seas. It is estimated that one hundred to two hundred privateering enterprises set out from England every year throughout this period, averaging £150,000 to £300,000 per annum in Spanish booty.

Religious differences further added to this conflict, as the English leaders, in particular, sought to help their Protestant co-religionists in Holland gain independence from Catholic Spain. But such subtleties were lost upon the coarser spirits, as was revealed once fighting ceased in

A Spanish war-galley off a
Mediterranean port. The European
powers fought protracted wars against
Muslim corsairs. (National Maritime
Museum, Greenwich)

Above: A bow view of a seventeenth-century French war-galley.

1603. Many a privateer found himself abruptly unemployed and – having no peacetime skills – resentful at his fall from grace. Typical among these was John Ward, a fisherman who had joined Elizabeth's navy and risen through the ranks to command the ship *Lion's Whelp*.

When the war ended, he could be frequently heard complaining in the taverns of Portsmouth, reflecting upon past glories:

> 'Sblood, what would you have me say, where are the days that have been, and the seasons that we have seen, when we might sing, swear, drink, drab and kill men as freely as your cakemakers do flies? When we might do what we list, and the law would bear us out in't, nay when we might lawfully do that we shall be hanged for an we do now; when the whole sea was our empire, where we robbed at will, and the world but our garden where we walked for sport.

Completely given to the rover's life, Ward – like many another European mercenary – sought to continue his career by taking service with any master, including the Barbary corsairs.

The North African states of Algiers, Tunis and Tripoli had fought intermittently against Christian Europe for more than eight centuries, until such confrontations had become a routine way of life for both sides. Although nominally controlled by the Sultans of remote Constantinople, real power was exercised in the Barbary states by each local Dey or Bey, elected by the military authorities of their district.

In addition to their obvious religious motivation, the Barbary corsairs had also come to depend upon privateering for their economic well-being. In particular, both Muslim and Christian raiders plundered one another's vessels for goods and hostages, the latter to be held for ransom, or used as slaves. (One such unfortunate, who suffered five years' incarceration at Algiers from 1575 to 1580, was the Spaniard Miguel de Cervantes, later author of *Don Quixote*.) This taking of slaves remained a necessary expedient when the principal type of warship available to either side was the galley. Of ancient design, these vessels were relatively well adapted to the enclosed, shallow waters of the Mediterranean, but required a steady supply of oarsmen.

The typical Muslim galley measured 180 feet in length by sixteen in breadth, with a single mast. The greater part of its space was taken up by banks of chained rowers, who plied fifteen-foot oars. The main armament was light, consisting of a large gun or two in the bows behind a massive ram, as the corsairs preferred taking prizes by manoeuvring into an oblique position, then closing to board. After clearing the enemy's decks with a point-blank blast from their heavy artillery, fighting men would scramble across with muskets and scimitars, overpowering their opponents in hand-to-hand combat.

Command of a Muslim galley was exercised by a *rais* or captain, generally a Turk or European renegade, who often owned his ship as well. The combatants, as many as 150 in number, would be directed by an Agha of Janizaries, the soldiers themselves being trusted slaves raised in a martial tradition under the tenets of Islam, and who had once been fabled for their ferocity and skill. The brothers Barbarossa, for instance, two Greeks of humble origin more properly known as Aruj and Khair-ed-Din, had terrorised the Mediterranean with just such a seagoing force during the first half of the sixteenth century.

By the early seventeenth century, however, the Janizaries' fearsome reputation had been considerably blunted, both by their crushing defeat at the hands of a combined Spanish–Venetian fleet at Lepanto in October 1571, as well as their incessant attrition in the Ottoman empire's two-front war against Austria and Persia. For this reason, when vast numbers of Christian privateers such as Ward were made idle by the cessation of the Elizabethan

wars, they found ready employment in North Africa. By 1606, the Sieur de Brèves was reporting on the startling sight of English corsairs at Algiers, saying that 'they run drunk through the town [and] in brief, every kind of debauchery and unchecked licence is permitted to them'. The Muslim leaders required the infidels' fighting skill and expertise, so were prepared to overlook such excesses for a while.

Certainly Ward came to prosper under the Dey of Tunis' service, within a short span of time commanding a fleet of ten ships. By 1609 he was among the most feared corsair captains anywhere in the Mediterranean, and the subject of numerous ballads and pamphlets in London, which decried his un-Christianlike faith while at the same time enviously describing his residence as 'a very stately house in Tunis, rich with marble and alabaster, more fit for a prince than a pirate'. He eventually converted to Islam, taking the name Yusuf Rais.

Another prominent European mercenary who served the Barbary cause was a German or Dutchman known as Simon Danziger (or Dansker), who for a time had operated out of Marseilles as a privateer, before transferring to the service of the Dey of Algiers. Here his success quickly earned him the nickname Dali Rais – 'Captain Devil' – but eventually Danziger incurred the displeasure of his hosts by refusing to convert. By 1608 he was attempting to negotiate a return to France, where he had left his family. Sailing out of Algiers on an expedition, he captured a valuable Spanish galleon which instead of bringing back into that North African port, he carried to Marseilles. This treachery might have gone unpunished, had he not then foolishly visited Tunis in 1611 to ransom some captured French vessels, only to be taken up and hanged.

Yet the greatest contribution made by these rogue privateers was

not their individual depredations at sea, but rather their introduction of the North European 'round ship' to the Barbary seamen, as an alternative to the traditional galley. Its hardy design and superior handling qualities allowed the corsairs to extend their field of operations, by braving the heavier seas and greater distances of the open Atlantic. Soon the Moroccan port of Salé (outside the Straits of Gibraltar, near present-day Rabat) began to achieve prominence as an advance western base for piracy, and by the second decade of the seventeenth century Muslim raiders were roaming as far north as Devon and Cornwall, to land slaving parties and make off with men, women and children from these coastal villages.

In 1617 an entire fishing convoy returning to Dorset from the Grand Banks of Newfoundland was intercepted by Barbary men-o-war, and ten years later an even more dramatic coup was perpetrated by the renegade Dutch privateer Jan Jansz, known as Murad Rais: for he sailed as far as Iceland to plunder Reykjavik, seizing four hundred captives and an abundance of salt fish and hides. In 1631, another group of Barbary corsairs descended upon the town of Baltimore at the southernmost tip of Ireland, making away with more than one hundred slaves.

However, the mercenaries' tenure in Muslim service proved short-lived. On the one hand, the Barbary corsairs soon mastered their innovations, and so no longer needed the offensive, hard-drinking rovers themselves. On the other, the European marauders found all authoritarian rule stifling, and so preferred to seek their livelihood elsewhere. This decision was made all the easier by the fact that from far out across the ocean, a rich new continent beckoned – exotic and unexplored – where even pirates might become kings.

II

Brave New World

*The glitt'ring seeds, mother of fire, remained
Like golden sands, thick scattered on the shore
Of the wild deep, and shone in burning oar.*
Sir Richard Blackmore (1652–1729)

The first rovers to prowl the Antillean chain found its islands largely uninhabited, the Carib natives having been almost entirely exterminated by their exposure to European disease and weaponry, while most of the Spanish Conquistadors had then emigrated to the wealthier, more temperate climates of the mainland, such as the central highlands of the Viceroyalties of New Spain and Peru. Thus a vast tropical void had been left behind, into which streamed seamen of every nationality and description, hoping to trade, to poach or to steal from Spain's fast expanding empire.

Soon foreign smugglers began blatantly holding fairs in out-of-the-way estuaries, where they sold and bought tax-free cargoes through Spanish American intermediaries. The volume of this clandestine traffic became quite remarkable, it being recorded – in one particularly well-documented case – that from 1599 to 1605 no fewer than 768 foreign vessels called at Araya (on the northern coast of present–day Venezuela), either to gather salt from the local pans, or buy tobacco and pearls from its inhabitants. The northern

coasts of Hispaniola and south-eastern Cuba also became highly popular destinations, where a brisk trade developed in hides.

French hunters curing wild pig's meat in a West Indian smokehouse or *boucan*. These rugged individualists, crack shots capable of living off the land, proved impossible to eradicate by the Spaniards.

The Spanish Crown occasionally resorted to draconian measures in its attempts to stem this tide. On 2 August 1605, for example, the Governor of Santo Domingo appeared with 150 soldiers at the town of

Bayahá, on the north-western shores of that island, to read aloud a proclamation from Philip III. In it, the King complained of the 'inveterate and pernicious traffic' between foreign smugglers and the Spanish residents, directing that all households be transferred to the south coast, where such activities might be more closely monitored. The troops then put every building to the torch, along with those of nearby Puerto Plata, Monte Cristi and La Yaguana, despite the inhabitants' impassioned pleas. A Spanish battle-fleet under Admiral Luis Fajardo also called on this coast in January of the following year, to ensure the complete evacuation of its Spanish settlers.

But this 'scorched-earth' policy not only failed to discourage foreign interlopers, it actually provided them with a better foothold. Finding the farms abandoned and tens of thousands of cattle and pigs roaming freely throughout the hills, visiting seamen began to appropriate this territory for themselves. At first only tiny handfuls dotted the coastline – adventurers, castaways and deserters left behind by interloping ships, who eked out a meagre living hunting wild game. They cured their meat over low fires, on grills

14

made of green wood called *boucans* (from the Arawak Indian word *buccan*): hence their nickname of *boucaniers*, or buccaneers. They also bartered hides and tallow with passing vessels, to meet their other necessities.

Furthermore, large consortia began setting up outposts on other uninhabited islands, installing resident factors to conduct a better volume of business with Spanish America, and harvest supplemental cash crops (such as tobacco or sugar cane) by importing planters, indentured servants and slaves. The Spanish authorities sought to eradicate these encroachments and an undeclared, low-grade warfare gradually evolved, of seaborne raid and counter-raid. The European trespassers resorted to their old familiar tactics from commercial warfare, by intercepting Spanish vessels and carrying these off, as well as landing to secure captives and plunder on shore. To the bitterness of territorial disputes was added the religious intolerance of that day, as many of these interlopers were Protestant, an affront to pious Spaniards who had hoped to keep the New World free of heresy.

The Dutch were especially active in these early clashes, having emerged victorious from their war of independence against Spain, and now bent upon expanding their burgeoning trade overseas. When hostilities resumed between these two powers in 1621 (after a hiatus known as the Twelve-Year Truce), numerous Dutch expeditions entered the Caribbean and added to the general fighting. Pieter Schouten, for example, led a three-ship reconnaissance force through

Right: Dutch engraving of the interception of the Mexican treasure fleet off Matanzas, Cuba, by Piet Heyn and his Vice-Admiral Hendrick Corneliszoon Loncq, in September 1628. Note that the insert shows both the islands of Cuba and Jamaica upside down.

the West Indies in 1624, ransacking the towns of Zilam and Sisal on the northern coast of Yucatán, as well as capturing one of the rich Spanish galleons trafficking with Honduras.

The following September Boudewijn Hendricksz attacked San Juan de Puerto Rico with fourteen sail, landing seven to eight hundred soldiers and besieging its citadel, only to be repulsed with heavy losses. In September 1628, the 51-year-old

Above: Imaginary view of the roads at Havana, terminus for the Spanish plate fleets.

Pieter Pieterszoon Heyn – better known to history as Piet Heyn – more than made up for this setback by capturing an entire Mexican treasure convoy off Matanzas on the northern shores of Cuba. His expedition was huge, consisting of

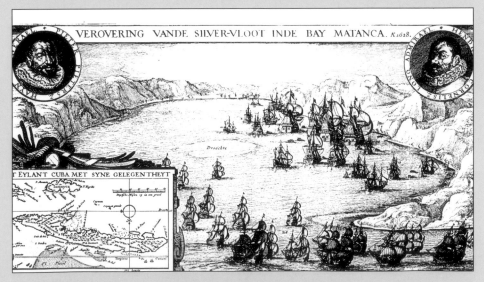

31 ships mounting 679 cannon, manned by 2,300 sailors and one thousand soldiers, yet still showed an astounding profit of more than seven million guilders following his return to Holland with this spectacular haul. Such a coup naturally encouraged other rovers.

The Spaniards responded by dispatching a battle-fleet under Admiral Fadrique de Toledo into the Caribbean the following year, which materialised unexpectedly off the British island of Nevis on 17 September 1629, capturing its colonists and eight vessels anchored offshore. Two days later, a like treatment was visited upon Saint Christopher (St Kitts) which was jointly shared by French and British settlers. Admiral de Toledo forcibly deported two thousand Englishmen to their homeland aboard six ships, while carrying away another eight hundred – who had agreed to convert to Catholicism and swear fealty to Philip IV – towards Cartagena. Still, the lure of the West Indies was much too strong to be blunted by such isolated reprisals, and these two islands were soon reoccupied by more foreigners.

On 16 February 1630, a Dutch fleet under Adriaen Janszoon Pater overran Santa Marta on the Spanish Main (in present-day Colombia), occupying it for a week before withdrawing upon receipt of a ransom of 5,500 *reales* – a not uncommon practice in European warfare of that time, where the Thirty Years War was in full swing, and whose brutal dictates were already being emulated in New World conflicts. Ever more powerful squadrons of privateers continued to prowl the Caribbean for the next three years, until the ten-vessel fleet of Jan Janszoon van Hoorn captured the Central American port of Trujillo on 15 July 1633. Disappointed by its scanty spoils, he sailed away six days later with the intention of attacking the Mexican port of Campeche, on the far side of the Yucatán peninsula.

Although no Dutch raider had yet penetrated this deep into the Gulf of Mexico, Van Hoorn had been encouraged in his plan by a mulatto pirate named Diego de los Reyes, born a slave in Havana, Cuba, only to flee his master and become a successful rover known to his Spanish–American victims as Diego the Mulatto, or sometimes Diego Lucifer. Having once resided at Campeche himself, De los Reyes was thoroughly familiar with its roadstead and defences, so led the way.

Towards noon on Friday, 11 August 1633, the inhabitants of this city beheld the thirteen sail of Van Hoorn and De los Reyes bearing down upon them, and next morning 'there emerged on to land more than five hundred troops of different nationalities', according to one terrified Spanish eye-witness, 'Dutchmen, Englishmen, Frenchmen and a few Portuguese' who advanced against Campeche's defences under Diego the Mulatto and Van Hoorn's most famed subordinate, peg-legged Captain Cornelis Corneliszoon Jol (pronounced 'Yol' in English). Although a cluster of armed boats covered their approach from offshore, the raiders' initial assault was repelled by fifty arquebusiers under Captain Domingo Galván Romero, entrenched along the western circuit of the city with three artillery pieces.

But when this assault column broke and fled, the defenders foolishly rose from their trenches and set off in pursuit, only to be trapped in open countryside once the attackers reformed. The brave Galván was shot down, and the way into Campeche lay open. (Local legend has it that De los Reyes knelt beside his body to mutter a brief prayer, as the two had once been friends.) The assault force then poured directly into the city streets,

Captain Ruy Fernández de Fuenmayor. Under cover of darkness, this combined force stole down upon Tortuga Island the night of 21 January, determined to wipe out this lawless settlement, which had been increasingly preying upon Spanish shipping.

Guided by an Irish lad named John Murphy, who had recently fled that buccaneer colony after killing a man in a dispute, the Spaniards disembarked through its treacherous surf and took the three hundred inhabitants completely by surprise. Anthony Hilton, the self-proclaimed British 'governor', was slain together with 194 of his followers, and another 39 including three women were captured. Its six-gun battery was also thrown down, two prizes in the harbour burnt, and another sailed back to Santo Domingo by the victorious Spaniards, laden with 123 captured muskets and a great deal of ammunition.

However, they neglected to leave any garrison behind, so that the remaining buccaneers soon reoccupied their base. This same year a Dutch West India Company expedition under Jan van Walbeeck and Pierre le Grand seized the island of Curaçao as an advance depot for their trade, further solidifying this country's presence in the Caribbean. Such establishments, besides fomenting an ever increasing clandestine traffic, also served the local privateers as safe havens for refurbishment and resupply, without which they could not have functioned. On 3 March 1635, the crippled Jol – already feared throughout the Spanish Indies by his nickname *Pie de Palo* (literally, 'Wooden Leg') – became one of the first corsairs to sortie from

unchecked until it encountered another three hundred Spaniards drawn up in the main square. A ferocious firefight ensued, ending with more than three dozen Spanish dead and many more captives, while the terrified survivors retreated in the direction of nearby San Francisco Campechuelo.

Van Hoorn, Jol and De los Reyes remained in possession of Campeche for the next two days, and although they stripped it of everything of value and seized 22 vessels lying in its roads, they were unable to extort any ransoms out of the interior. They therefore spiked its guns and sailed a dozen miles up

the coast before releasing their captives, retaining nine prizes while selling another four back to the Spaniards, and burning the rest. Van Hoorn then returned triumphantly toward Holland, while Jol and De los Reyes went their separate ways, continuing to inflict punishment upon the Spanish–Americans.

Not that the latter were incapable of retaliating. On 4 January 1634, four Spanish warships slipped out of the capital of Santo Domingo under Captain Francisco Turrillo de Yelva, circling around that island to rendezvous with 150 soldiers who had marched overland to Bayahá under

Opposite page: Detail of a Spanish painting celebrating the defeat of Boudewijn Hendricksz's attempted invasion of San Juan de Puerto Rico, in November 1625. Note that the painter Eugenio Caxés has symbolically depicted some Dutch attackers wearing orange. (El Prado Museum, Madrid).

Right: Imaginary Dutch view of Trujillo, Honduras, as it appeared in the seventeenth century

Curaçao, on one of his boldest strokes.

Accompanied by only the ship *Brack* ('Beagle') of Captain Cornelis Janszoon van Uytgeest, Jol's *Otter* penetrated the narrow confines of the roadstead at Santiago de Cuba, both ships masquerading as Spanish merchantmen. In addition to flying false colours, the two Dutch captains elaborated upon their deception by disguising some of their deck-hands as Spanish friars. When Santiago's pilot-boat drew near to welcome these new arrivals, its officers belatedly perceived their enemies' true identity, yet had already come so close as to be fired upon and captured.

A heated exchange then erupted with the shore batteries, during which Jol had the half-dozen merchantmen lying in the roads searched, finding most empty. During a lull in the firing he coolly offered to ransom these and his prisoners, to which the Spanish governor haughtily refused, so that the battle raged on until evening. Getting under way with the land

breeze, Jol and Van Uytgeest then had the good fortune to encounter a fully laden, inbound Spanish frigate while clearing the mouth of the bay, which they seized before making off. They then unloaded and burnt this prize, releasing all their captives two days later.

Jol was to sow even greater terror throughout the West Indies that summer, capturing at least another ten large Spanish ships. By the time he set sail for Holland that autumn, *Otter* was carrying more than two thousand hides, two and a half tons of tobacco, two tons of sarsaparilla, as well as a great deal of silver and other produce. But within sight of his homeland he suffered the ignominy of being captured by a squadron of Dunkirk privateers under Jacques Colaert, who towed his ship into that anchorage on 2 November 1635; both commander and crew remained incarcerated in the Spanish Netherlands for the next nine months.

Jol's bad luck persisted even after he was exchanged and returned to the West Indies with a strong

squadron of privateers in late 1636. After fruitlessly hunting for prizes off Île-à-Vache (near the south-western tip of present-day Haiti) for several months, the rover led his forces to Cartagena, where he sighted a powerful treasure fleet standing out of that bay towards Havana on 3 August 1637. These 26 proud Spanish galleons proved much too formidable to be tackled head-on by Jol's smaller craft, and when one straggler lagged behind, a number of his and other local privateers became so embroiled in laying claim to this one vessel, that the Spaniard was able to make good his escape. Jol complained bitterly of the indiscriminate issuing of commissions by the Dutch West India Company at Curaçao, which had resulted in such an ill-disciplined display.

These frequent hostilities had served as a magnet, attracting ever more seaborne mercenaries into the Caribbean arena. One such veteran corsair still operating under Dutch licence was Jol's former partner from Campeche, Diego the Mulatto. The English Catholic priest and

Buccaneer Tactics

At the height of their powers during the latter half of the seventeenth century, privateers often agreed to combine their forces to launch major land strikes, rather than merely intercept individual vessels on the high seas. This amphibious ability had been developed early on, during the 1650s and 1660s, when many of their first campaigns included veteran soldiers who had been resettled in the Antilles, and thus constituted a ready pool of experienced volunteers. The latter's martial qualities not only made them valuable fighters, but their familiarity with past brutalities from the Thirty Years War, English Civil War, Franco–Spanish War and other such conflicts, meant that they were well suited to piratical campaigns in the New World, where plunder was always a primary objective.

Nevertheless the battle-discipline of these early formations must not be under-estimated, as numerous eye-witnesses have attested: for example, armies such as Morgan's frequently marched into action in serried ranks, 'with drums beating and banners flying'. Such cohesiveness allowed the buccaneers to confront much larger Spanish–American units and defeat them, thanks largely to their superior firepower.

Even after this initial blush of martial prowess began to fade, the buccaneers persisted with these same basic tactics for another couple of decades. Usually, a group of licensed rovers would muster at some remote locale, obtaining detailed intelligence about an unsuspecting coastal target. They would then use their vessels to approach this place unseen, disembark nearby and advance stealthily to attack at dawn (whenever possible on a Sunday, further to surprise their quarry). This assault would inevitably be loud, abrupt and confusing, with lots of gunfire and noise to overwhelm any resistance before it could develop, thereby minimising the pirates' casualties while at the same time paralysing their potential victims before these could flee.

Prisoners would be quickly herded into a single place (usually the largest church), while buildings and warehouses were ransacked and booty gathered into a general pile, to be removed to the ships arriving from offshore. Wealthy captives would be tortured to reveal their hidden treasures, after which ransom demands would be sent inland for their release, as well as to spare the city further destruction upon the raiders' withdrawal. Within a few days, before relief columns could arrive to challenge the buccaneers, they would retire with as many black and Indian inhabitants as possible, intending to sell these as slaves in the Antillean marts. A final distribution of plunder would then be made at some prearranged rendezvous, after which the buccaneers would disperse and dispose of their booty privately, wherever each commander or crew saw fit.

One such example was offered in the summer of 1678 by the English privateer George Spurre, operating under a French commission. On 10 April of that year he was prowling off the north-western Cuban coast with his frigate and the sloop of Edward Neville, a total of 105 men between them, when they sighted the Spanish dispatch vessel *Toro* ('Bull') out of Havana bound for Veracruz. Intercepting this ship, they carried her into the Santa Isabel cays, where Spurre scuttled his frigate and transferred aboard *Toro*. All the Spaniards except their pilot were released at Bahía Honda, the buccaneers retaining this specialist for his detailed knowledge of the Gulf of Mexico.

Spurre and Neville crossed to the Laguna de Términos in New Spain, capturing the ketch of Alvaro Sánchez *en route*. From their prisoners they had learnt enough about the approaches and defences of Campeche to essay an attack, and therefore spent the next three weeks in the Laguna recruiting additional men for this enterprise. The two commanders were careful to select only the best individuals from a throng of volunteers, raising their total strength to 180 men, although Spurre later boasted to a Spanish captive that 'if he had wished, he could have collected up to four hundred men for the sack'.

Once ready, the expedition ventured north-eastward aboard their two ships, towing eight *piraguas* astern. They circled past Campeche and anchored near Jaina, whence Neville departed on the night of 6/7 July 1678 to reconnoitre the port from his sloop. He rejoined the main body at daybreak, reporting that all was calm within the Spanish

traveller Thomas Gage confirmed this fact when his tiny Spanish coaster was boarded by De los Reyes and another Dutch privateer off the Costa Rican coast during this same year of 1637. The buccaneers stripped it of everything of value, and when Gage complained to the pirate captain, Diego airily replied by 'using that common proverb at sea – *Hoy por mi, mañana por ti* – today fortune hath been for me, tomorrow it may be for thee.' None the less the Mulatto released his captives unharmed, adding to his general reputation for magnanimity. (That previous year Diego had also intercepted a vessel off Mexico bearing Doña Isabel de Caraveo, recently widowed from the Governor of Yucatán, whom he had chivalrously restored to shore with all her goods.)

In 1638, after visiting Holland, Jol returned into the West Indies with yet another strong formation of privateers, but on meeting the Cartagena treasure convoy of Admiral Carlos de Ibarra off the north coast of Cuba early in September, his captains failed to press home their attack, and the Spanish emerged victorious. The peg-legged chieftain retired across the Atlantic once more, and never returned to these hunting grounds. He died three years later while capturing the Portuguese slaving station of São Tomé off West Africa, and no more large Dutch expeditions swept through the Caribbean. Instead their West India Company had harbour. That evening the two captains slipped ashore with 160 pirates, leaving instructions for their anchor watches to bear down upon Campeche at dawn two days later. If twin smoke columns could be seen, this would signify that the town had been won and they could enter the roads.

The landing-party meanwhile approached Campeche by nocturnal stages, capturing every person they chanced to meet. Some of these were tortured to reveal the best access to the town, and an Indian named Juan 'was tied up and threatened to have his head cut off by a cutlass which the pirate captain showed him', if he did not agree to lead them into the city. An hour before daybreak on Sunday, 10 July, the column of buccaneers materialised before a small city gate, where their terrified captive answered the sentinel's challenge and gained them access.

In the gloom, the sentry had assumed these shadowy figures were a group of Indians come for market-day, after which the attackers marched swiftly towards the central plaza, ignoring the few startled churchgoers preparing for mass. Once in front of the Governor's residence, the column was challenged again, but this time 'the pirates with a great shout fired a heavy volley'. Campeche's garrison was taken utterly by surprise, only nine soldiers being on duty instead of the requisite sixty. (Moreover, its best troops – the town's mulatto militia – were absent on patrol against bandits in the surrounding hills, which Spurre and Neville doubtless knew full well.)

The garrison commander, or *sargento mayor*, Gonzalo Borrallo, was so shocked that he vaulted over his back wall armed only with a sword and clad in his night-shirt, but after being fired at repeatedly 'from point-blank range' out of the darkness, retreated to his house where he was seized. Virtually every prominent citizen shared this same fate, the only Spaniards to escape being the four-man watch aboard Juan Ramírez's frigate in the roads. These got their vessel under way after hearing the first reports, and cleared the harbour, a sight which so infuriated the buccaneers that they turned upon Ramírez – whom they held captive – and savagely hacked him to death, 'giving him many sword thrusts and cutting off his nose'.

Toro and Neville's sloop duly appeared on schedule, two huts being fired down by the waterfront to signal them to enter. Other Spaniards were terrified into raising ransoms, and every building was thoroughly ransacked during the next few days. Although the freebooters only held Campeche until the evening of Tuesday the 12th, they withdrew with considerable loot: the ship *San Antonio*, a *barco luengo* and a boat, as well as money and foodstuffs. They also carried off 250 black, mulatto and Indian townspeople to sell as slaves at the Laguna de Términos, all for negligible losses.

By that autumn, William Beeston was noting in his journal at Port Royal, Jamaica:

> 18 October 1678 [O.S.]. Arrived Captain Splure [*sic*; Spurre], who with one Neville about three months since, and 150 men, had taken Campeche, and with him a prize; for all of which he had his pardon, and leave to come in and spend their plunder.

The number of such hit-and-run raids was simply staggering. Within the next four years, a Spanish inhabitant of Cartagena would disconsolately observe that:

> Trinidad has been robbed once; Margarita and Guayana burnt once and sacked twice; La Guaira, sacked once and its inhabitants sold ... [Pirates also] entered Puerto Cabello and sacked Valencia, which is more than twenty leagues inland. Maracaibo has been robbed many times ... the city of Ríohacha abandoned, the city and garrison of Santa Marta sacked more than three times and burnt once ...

This list would soon come to include ports on the Pacific coast, as rapacious buccaneers pushed across the Isthmus of Panama in search of fresher prey.

But this relentless storm of land assaults would eventually begin to wane as the century drew to a close, with better coastal defences being erected, sanctuaries denied, and the buccaneers themselves losing their appetite for such martial exercises. By the early eighteenth century few soldiers were being recruited for their ventures, the bulk of the rovers being – as in early days – disgruntled sailors eager to seek rich prizes at sea, rather than operate on land. The day of the buccaneer was past.

deemed these unprofitable, and future hostilities were conducted mostly by local privateers, operating out of Curaçao.

In one such enterprise, four Dutch men-of-war and two sloops under Hendrik Gerristz entered the Laguna de Maracaibo on 16 October 1641, bypassing that city to fall upon the town of San Antonio de Gibraltar at the south-eastern extremity of this same body of water. Two hundred raiders quickly disembarked and stripped its outlying districts of their tobacco and cacao harvests, bombarding Maracaibo as they withdrew from the Laguna two weeks later. The provincial Governor at Caracas, Ruy Fernández de Fuenmayor (the same individual who had surprised the buccaneer lair of Tortuga Island seven years earlier), responded by overrunning the Dutch island of Bonaire with three hundred soldiers on 1 October 1642, leaving it temporarily depopulated.

But only a few months later, yet another formidable opponent appeared to bedevil the Spaniards, this time in the form of a British squadron. William Jackson had quit England with three men-of-war to avenge the Spanish extermination of their intruder settlement on Providencia Island eighteen months previously, in which 770 British captives had been carried off into bondage. Touching first at St Kitts and Barbados, Jackson had found these colonies so abundantly estab-

Spanish warships. (National Maritime Museum, Greenwich)

lished that he had been able to raise his total strength to a dozen vessels and more than one thousand men, simply by calling for volunteers.

In conjunction with these reinforcements, he assaulted Caracas' port of La Guaira in early December 1642, only to be ejected by Fernández de Fuenmayor and the warlike bishop of that city, Mauro de Tovar (suitably attired in an armoured breastplate). Unfazed by this setback, Jackson then bombarded Maiquetía and Puerto Cabello in quick succession, before penetrating into the Laguna de Maracaibo on 23 December and landing eight hundred men, who took this city by surprise. The British remained in occupation of Maracaibo until 1 February 1643, when they traversed the Laguna to lay waste the countryside outside Gibraltar, although this town proved too well prepared to be stormed.

Upon retiring from the Laguna, Jackson and his eleven-vessel mercenary squadron paused at the island of Jamaica on Good Friday 1643, where he landed five hundred men and remained for more than a month. Its unprepossessing capital of Santiago de la Vega was spared in exchange for a tiny ransom, after which the invaders sailed away, homeward bound. Although he found England engulfed in civil war on his return, Jackson's expedition presaged his country's rise as a major Caribbean player. Within five years the Dutch would sign a peace treaty with Spain, and although their seamen continued to be highly active in these waters for the remainder of the century, their government henceforth pursued a commercial rather than a confrontational policy regarding Spanish America.

France remained at war with Spain, but would not be free from its internal and continental entanglements to concentrate on Antillean developments for some decades to come. England, too,

Arquebusier.

remained distracted for a period by its Civil War, yet emerged sufficiently invigorated under its new republican leader, Oliver Cromwell, to challenge Holland for primacy at sea. The First Anglo–Dutch War erupted as a result in the spring of 1652, and engrossed the full attention of these two maritime powers for the next couple of years.

Spain meanwhile continued its long, sad decline, and no longer had the strength even to mount expeditions to beat back foreign poachers from the West Indies. A few local raids out of Puerto Rico sought to contain the more noticeable enemy advances in the neighbouring Virgin Islands, the rest of the Leeward and Windward Islands having already been given up for lost. In May of 1650, four Cuban warships with 350 troops under Captain Francisco de Villalba y Toledo unsuccessfully assaulted the British buccaneering camps on the

island of Roatan (in the Gulf of Honduras), but were forced to withdraw when their ammunition ran low. Resupplied and reinforced by an additional one hundred soldiers from Guatemala, De Villalba returned to this attack in late July, but although he overran Roatan on this second attempt, he took no prisoners and its elusive buccaneers simply resettled after he had retired to Cuba.

One of the last noteworthy Spanish successes of this era occurred on Tortuga Island north of Hispaniola, which had been held for the past decade by a colony of French and British *boucaniers* under François Le Vasseur. During this interval he had constructed a large stone fortress with 44 guns which commanded its principal harbour. From this stronghold his pirates had become increasingly bold, sacking the frontier town of Santiago de los Caballeros on Santo Domingo's mainland in 1650, then descending upon the hapless Cuban port of San Juan de los Remedios in August 1652. Shortly thereafter Le Vasseur was assassinated by some French rivals, but Tortuga's buccaneers continued to be a thorn in the Spaniards' side.

Consequently, a punitive expedition of five vessels slipped out of the capital of Santo Domingo on 4 December 1653, bearing two hundred soldiers and five hundred volunteers. These were commanded by Captain Gabriel de Rojas y Figueroa, seconded by the former Irish renegade John Murphy (who in the intervening twenty years had been promoted *maestre de campo* or second in command of that colony's militia, as well as invested with a knighthood in the Order of Santiago). On the 20th they reached Puerto Plata where two of their ships ran aground and had to be left behind; all their passengers were transferred to the other three, which proceeded towards Monte Cristi.

While approaching this harbour they encountered a trio of buccaneer craft, which in the expectation of encountering lightly armed merchantmen closed rapidly, only to sheer off in fright once they detected the Spaniards' crowded decks. One of De Rojas's ships ran aground in pursuit of these fleeing pirates, but another effectively cut off their escape, forcing the buccaneers to beach their ships and flee into the jungle. The Spanish were then unable to refloat their own vessel or one of the prizes, but manned the other two and continued towards Tortuga aboard these four ships.

Its garrison saw the Spaniards bearing down upon them at midday on 9 February 1654, gliding past the harbour and bombarding the vessels anchored in its roads. Three miles farther along the coast, opposite the hamlet of Cayenne, the Spaniards disembarked several hundred troops and marched back to besiege its principal fortress. On the night of the 12th, Rojas sent a large party of men with grappling lines to scale the heights behind this place, and install siege artillery. By the 18th the French were so battered and starved as to request terms, and two days later surrendered. More than five hundred captives were taken, among them 330 *boucaniers*.

All save two hostage leaders were allowed to sail for France aboard a pair of ships, while the Spanish took stock of their booty: seventy cannon in the fortress and shore batteries, three ships, a frigate and eight lesser craft. Furthermore, on this occasion they also decided to hold on to their hard-won conquest, by leaving behind a garrison of one hundred troops under Murphy. A few months later the authorities on Santo Domingo sent Captain Baldomero Calderón Espinosa with 150 soldiers to relieve him, as they still did not fully trust the Irishman out of their sight.

Thus the Spaniards were still in possession when five pirate vessels returned to Tortuga on 24 August 1654, hoping to reoccupy their island. These included a contingent of the original French settlers, who had sailed only as far as St Kitts and recruited more followers, and now landed intent on giving battle. After eight days' fruitless combat they were forced to re-embark, and opposite Monte Cristi were intercepted by three Spanish men-of-war hastening to Tortuga's rescue. One buccaneer ship with fifty men aboard was captured, half of them being Dutch and the remainder French. The former were spared and carried prisoner into Santo Domingo, the latter were hanged from the yardarms for violating their parole.

Nevertheless another expedition was already marshalling far out across the Atlantic, which would not only dwarf such actions, but unalterably affect the spread of privateering in the West Indies. The First Anglo–Dutch War had ceased in the spring of that year, so that in England Oliver Cromwell was now free to pursue his considerable ambitions overseas. Weary of Spanish intransigence and convinced that England must secure a major foothold in the West Indies to rival Holland's profits from New World trade, the Protector opted for a daring conquest of Santo Domingo, despite the uneasy peace prevailing with Madrid. As a result, seventeen warships and 21 transports stood out of Portsmouth on 24 December 1654 (Old Style, the calendar used by the British but not by most other European powers) under Admiral William Penn, with 2,500 regulars under General Robert Venables.

These reached Barbados 35 days later, where a convoy of victuallers awaited them, and 3,500 volunteers were then raised from among the islands over the next two months to supplement the troops brought out from England. Finally, the whole expedition materialised before Santo Domingo in late April 1655, and while Penn bore down menacingly upon the defences to create a diversion, Vice-Admiral William Goodson led the bulk of the fleet westward, seeking a disembarkation point. However, because of uncertainty regarding the shoals, he deposited this army thirty miles away, an absurdly long distance which contributed to the eventual defeat of this enterprise.

The troops spent the next several days struggling back through the jungle, while the outnumbered Spaniards recovered from their initial shock and beat off the enfeebled British assaults, until the invaders were forced to withdraw with the loss of one thousand men, chiefly due to disease. Hoping to salvage something from this unexpected fiasco, the British commanders then turned their attentions on smaller Jamaica, landing unopposed there that May. They quickly dispersed its few Spanish inhabitants, who either evacuated the island altogether, or inaugurated a guerrilla warfare out of its trackless interior.

As the sick-lists continued to mount, Penn immediately prepared to return to England, leaving Goodson – until recently a well-to-do Puritan supplier for the navy – as overall commander of nine small men-of-war and four converted victuallers, his flag flying aboard the State's ship *Torrington*. The main body departed in early July 1655, and it soon became apparent that the doughty Goodson was ill suited for the wiles of West Indian campaigns. Such skills soon became necessary as neighbouring Spanish–American colonies had already begun harassing raids against the intrusive British settlement, which called for some sort of retaliation.

In his first attempt, Goodson sailed for the Spanish Main one month later, leaving a few ships on station to help defend Jamaica. Having tacked 450 miles upwind to Santa Marta, he took, sacked and burned this town, although so unimaginatively as to accomplish little and secure scant booty. Moving openly down the coast towards Cartagena, he looked in to this port – although knowing full well that his force was insufficient to attempt it – before returning to Jamaica empty-handed by mid-November 1655 'to refit and consider of some other design'.

During that winter he was joined by 36-year-old Christopher Myngs, who brought out the warship *Marston Moor* from England on 25 January 1656. That spring Goodson again ventured towards the Main, sailing from Jamaica with a diminished force (although this time including Myngs) to fall upon Ríohacha that May. After devastating this place – again for little profit – he made his way aimlessly down the coast to water at Santa Marta, before again anchoring impotently off Cartagena for a day, then returning to Jamaica by early June 1656. Equally unsuccessful attempts followed against the Spanish plate fleets, until Goodson finally transferred into *Mathias* in January 1657, and sailed away for England complaining of ill health.

His subordinate Myngs followed a month later with a three-ship convoy, bringing *Marston Moor* into Dover in July 1657 after a brief stop at the Bahamas to buy 8,560 pounds of turtle meat for food. His crew were paid off and Myngs was allowed leave of absence to get married, but by December was back on board, departing the Downs with three victuallers, again bound for Jamaica. He arrived on 20 February 1658 (O.S.), having captured *en route* six Dutch merchantmen for illegally trading at the British island of Barbados. He claimed all six as prizes, but was annoyed when eventually only one was so adjudged, the rest being released on technicalities.

Myngs was now the senior officer on that station, and at last able to exercise his flair for independent command. His tenure began promisingly when four Spanish troop transports were discovered at anchor off the north coast of that island on 22 May 1658, having slipped 550 Mexican soldiers ashore. Returning a month later with Governor Edward d'Oyley and heavy reinforcements aboard ten ships, Myngs was able to land this force, which then pulverised the invaders in a pitched battle. The Spanish artillery was conveyed back to Cagway (as the island capital was still called), and installed as part of its harbour defences.

Shortly thereafter Myngs sailed in his first operation against the Main, assaulting Santa Marta and Tolú in quick succession with the loss of only three men, then intercepting three Spanish merchantmen bound from Cartagena to Portobelo. Returning triumphantly to Jamaica six weeks later, he sold all three to men who would eventually prove formidable corsairs: the largest vessel, of eight guns and sixty tons, was bought by Robert Searle and renamed *Cagway*; one of four guns and fifty tons was purchased by the Dutch-born Laurens Prins and renamed *Pearl*; while the third later became John Morris's *Dolphin*.

Having enjoyed such good success on his first cruises, Myngs's frigates *Marston Moor*, *Hector* and *Cagway* were joined by numerous freebooters for his next raid against the Main, which he launched early the following year. This time, in order to surprise some unsuspecting targets, he patiently tacked hundreds of miles farther east than he or Goodson

Myngs's Campaign Against the Spanish Main (Spring 1659): After repeated descents (dotted line) against the western portions of the Spanish Main by Commodore Goodson in 1655 and 1656, as well as Myngs himself in 1658, the latter adopted a more cunning strategy. Reinforced by a sizeable contingent of privateers, he beat a thousand miles upwind to fall upon unsuspecting Cumaná (1); after ransacking this port, he quickly weighed and hurried downwind to visit a like treatment upon Puerto Cabello (2) and Coro (3), before either could receive any warning overland. He thus secured an unusually large amount of booty.

Right: Allegorical depiction of English soldiers landing on an Antillean isle.

Above: Scene of a bombardment of the English settlements on Roatan by Spanish warships, during the eighteenth century. (Archivo General de Indias, Seville, Spain)

had ever previously operated. This paid handsome dividends when his formation burst upon an unprepared Cumaná, seizing and ransacking this port. Myngs then hurriedly weighed and ran westward before the prevailing winds, falling upon Puerto Cabello before

any alarm could be carried overland by the first Spanish victims. He repeated this tactic a third time, by racing still farther west to make a rich haul at Coro.

It was in the roads at this latter place that no less than 22 chests, and perhaps many more, were seized from two Dutch merchantmen flying Spanish colours, each containing four hundred pounds of silver ingots belonging to the King of Spain. Myngs himself afterwards declared that there was 'coined [*i.e.*, minted] money' in these chests to

the value of £50,000, besides bullion; but when his expedition returned to Jamaica these were found broken open, and the Protectorate's authorities suspected a great deal of silver had been purloined.

Myngs did not deny that some looting had been allowed to occur, but dismissed it as customary among privateersmen after the heat of battle. The officials took a dimmer view, believing that Myngs was 'unhinged and out of tune' because the Jamaican court had earlier refused to condemn his Dutch prizes, and so was taking justice into his own hands. Governor D'Oyley consequently suspended him and ordered *Marston Moor* home, where Myngs was to stand trial for defrauding the State.

But upon his arrival in England in the spring of 1660, Myngs found the entire nation distracted by the Restoration of Charles II, and – being an early public supporter of the monarch – was soon cleared of all charges after a sympathetic hearing that June. By the end of that year he was restored to command, and began making ready for a third tour of duty on the Jamaica station. Relations had also been patched up with Spain – yet ironically, only now was the Golden Age of Piracy about to commence.

III

No Peace Beyond the Line

Now sing the triumphs of the men of war.
Robert Wild (1609–1679)

In August 1662 there arrived at Port Royal the 40-gun frigate HMS *Centurion* under Myngs, bearing the first Royalist Governor for Jamaica, the 35-year-old Thomas, Lord Windsor. The latter's brief tenure in office would prove singularly important for privateering warfare in the West Indies, for even as he had been refreshing his supplies at Barbados that July following his trans-Atlantic crossing, Windsor had sent ahead his smaller consort, the 14-gun *Griffin*, with letters to the Spanish governors of Puerto Rico and Santo Domingo, asking if they would admit peaceful British merchantmen into their ports.

This seemingly innocuous request was actually a snare, for the British knew full well that the Spaniards had always rejected such overtures, despite the peace Madrid had signed only three years earlier with London. Indeed, during these latter negotiations the Spanish diplomats had steadfastly refused to even acknowledge England's presence in the New World, hoping eventually to reassert their monopoly over the entire continent. Now, in a bold attempt to breach this exclusionary policy, the new Jamaican governor was bringing out secret instructions from Charles II, that if 'the King of Spain shall refuse to admit our subjects to trade with them, you shall in such case endeavour to procure and settle a trade with his subjects in those parts by force'.

Windsor would find many willing spirits for this aggressive new strategy on Jamaica, for while still awaiting the Spanish Governor's reply, he swiftly began introducing

Seventeenth-century frigate.

other changes. Having brought out the back-pay for that colony's original Cromwellian garrison, he was able to release more than one thousand disgruntled soldiers from servitude, with full wages and a gratuity, replacing these with five volunteer militia regiments distributed throughout the island. Furthermore, a local assembly was convened and an Admiralty court established, so that henceforth Jamaica enjoyed a limited measure of autonomy, rather than always having to rely on decisions from the far side of the Atlantic. But his most surprising innovation followed the reappearance of the *Griffin* a few days later, with the expected Spanish rebuff.

Despite the peace prevailing back in Europe, Windsor immediately made privateering commissions available again on Jamaica 'for the subduing of all our enemies by sea and by land, within and upon the coast of America'. Shortly afterwards he also called for volunteers for a heavy strike against the Spaniards, to be led by Commodore Myngs. Many old hands were openly delighted at this bellicosity, so that within three days 1,300 men had mustered – most of them former soldiers – while *Centurion* and *Griffin* were joined by ten privateering vessels of various nationalities in the roads (including a tiny ship commanded by a 27-year-old militia captain named Henry Morgan).

Myngs was to lead these in a raid against Santiago de Cuba, which until recently had been the Spaniards' advance base in their efforts to reconquer Jamaica, and so

Right: A Dutch map of the West Indies.

bitterly resented by the British. His flotilla quit Port Royal on 1 October 1662, less than two months after he and the new Governor had arrived from England. Slowly rounding Point Negril at the west end of Jamaica in light winds, Myngs sighted the Cuban coast a few days later, where he encountered the ship of Sir Thomas Whetstone lying at anchor in the lee of a cay. The latter was an extraordinary rascal, having been nephew to the dead Oliver Cromwell, but remaining loyal to the Crown throughout the Civil War. In the heady days immediately following the Restoration of Charles II in 1660, Whetstone had got himself heavily into debt, being clapped into Marshalsea prison whence he was eventually released by the new King and received £100 to settle with his creditors, then emigrate to the New World. In the West Indies he had promptly turned pirate, commanding a 7-gun Spanish prize with a crew of 60 men, most of them renegade Indians.

Learning that Whetstone had been prowling that coast for some time, Myngs joined him at anchor to obtain the latest intelligence regarding Spanish dispositions. At a general conference held on board *Centurion*, the commodore decided to burst directly into that unsuspecting port, catching his prey by surprise. Reinforced by Whetstone and seven more Jamaican privateers who had belatedly overtaken his expedition, Myngs steered down the Cuban coast in scanty winds. His twenty vessels came within sight of the towering harbour castle guarding the entrance to Santiago at daybreak on 16 October, but could not rush the harbour mouth because of the faint, erratic breezes. Finally, late that afternoon Myngs decided to steer directly towards the nearby village of Aguadores, at the

mouth of the San Juan river, and by nightfall had succeeded in putting one thousand men ashore. In his own words:

We decided to land under a platform two miles to windward of the harbour, the only place possible to land and march upon the town on all that rocky coast. We found no resistance, the enemy expecting us at the fort and the people flying before us. Before we were all landed it was night. We were forced to advance into a wood, and the way was so narrow and difficult, and the night so dark, that our guides had to go with brands in their hands to beat a path. By daybreak we reached a plantation by a riverside, some six miles from our landing and three miles from the town where being refreshed by water, daylight and a better way, we very cheerfully advanced for the town, surprising the enemy who hearing our late landing, did not

expect us so soon. At the entrance of the town the Governor Don Pedro de Morales, with 200 men and two pieces of ordnance, stood to receive us, Don Christopher [de Issasi Arnaldo] the old Governor of [Spanish] Jamaica (and a good friend to the English) with 500 more being his reserve. We soon beat them from their station and with the help of Don Christopher, who fairly ran away, we routed the rest. Having mastered the town we took possession of the [seven] vessels in the harbour, and next day I dispatched parties in pursuit of the enemy and sent orders to the fleet to attack the harbour, which was successfully done, the enemy deserting the great castle after firing but two muskets.

Myngs spent the next five days pursuing the defeated Spaniards inland, 'which proved not very advantageous, their riches being drawn off so far we could not reach it'. Furious at being denied greater

plunder, the freebooters razed the town and Myngs used seven hundred barrels of gunpowder from the Spanish magazines to demolish the fortifications and principal buildings. After five days' calculated destruction, he was able to report:

The harbour castle mostly lies level with the ground. It was built upon a rocky precipice, the walls on a mountain side some 60 feet high; there was in it a chapel and houses sufficient for a thousand men.

It would take the Spaniards more than a decade to repair their devastated stronghold, and meanwhile Myngs returned triumphantly toward Port Royal, only to meet Windsor aboard the *Bear* heading home for England. The Governor claimed to be 'very sick and uneasy', but the real reason for his abrupt departure may have been financial rather than medical, as he later complained that 'he came back £2,000 worse off than when he went out'. This apparent abandoning of his royal duties was disapproved of when he reached London, Samuel Pepys noting in his diary: 'Lord Windsor being come home from Jamaica unlooked for, makes us think these young lords are not fit to do any service abroad.' But although he had been in office less than three months, Windsor none the less left two important precedents at Port Royal: one was his officially sanctioned hostility against the Spaniards, notwithstanding the peace prevailing in Europe; the other was his introduction of a local Assembly to that island, which could enact offensive measures of its own.

After Myngs brought his six prizes into harbour on 1 November, 'the privateers all went to sea for [more] plunder', according to a contemporary observer. They were elated by their easy success, this

Opposite page: As commander-in-chief of the Jamaica station, the bold and resourceful Christopher Myngs did much to set the precedent of large-scale seaborne descents against Spanish America during peacetime. Among those who learned their craft under him was a young Henry Morgan. (National Maritime Museum, Greenwich)

Right: Myngs's Assault against Santiago de Cuba (October 1662): At dawn on 16 October 1662, Myngs attempted to rush the harbour-mouth at Santiago de Cuba (dotted line), only to become becalmed (1). He therefore veered in towards the village of Aguadores that evening, landing one thousand men at the mouth of the San Juan River (2). Advancing inland during that night, he defeated a Spanish army before the city gates next morning (3), occupying Santiago and sending columns after its fleeing citizenry (4). Next day he dispatched another contingent to attack the harbour castle (5), which the Spaniards abandoned without a fight.

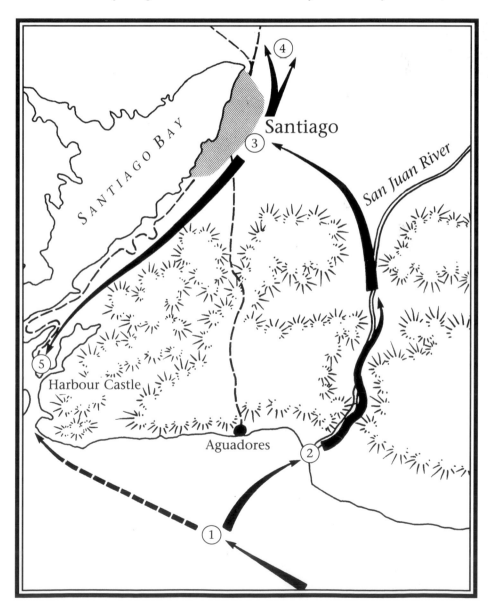

Griffin and several privateersmen, but none the less skilfully sneaked almost one thousand men ashore at Jámula beach, four miles west of his intended target, on the night of 8/9 February.

At first light the Spanish lookouts saw Myngs's smaller vessels clustered opposite this disembarkation point, with two large men-of-war riding farther out to sea. They sounded the alarm, but too late, as the freebooter army burst out of the nearby woods at 8 o'clock that morning and bore down upon the panic-stricken city. Despite being surprised and heavily outnumbered, the 150 Campeche militiamen put up a stout resistance, especially from their 'strong built stone houses, flat at top'. A bloody firefight ensued, in which Myngs received serious wounds in the face and both thighs while leading the opening charge up its principal street. He was carried back aboard *Centurion*, while Mansfield (in the absence of Myngs's Royal Naval subordinate, Smart) assumed overall command of the invading host. The Spanish defenders were eventually subdued after two hours' heated battle, suffering more than fifty fatalities as opposed to thirty attackers slain. Some 170 Spanish captives were then rounded up, while many of the city's thatched huts went up in flames.

The next morning a Spanish official entered and agreed to a truce, in exchange for good treatment of the prisoners. Despite his injuries, Myngs remained sufficiently in control to order the release of four prominent captives on 17 February, who carried a message to the Spaniards offering to spare their city and release the rest of their fellow-citizens, if the raiders could draw water from the nearby Lerma wells.

massive assault having cost only six men killed in the fighting and another twenty due to accidents or illness, while they also still held their commissions from Windsor. In the meantime Myngs found that he had been elected to the new Jamaican Council during his absence, which body decided to continue the departed Governor's confrontational policies. On 22 December it issued a call for a second punitive expedition against the Spaniards, so that freebooters of many different nations – although principally British, Dutch and Frenchmen – once again began marshalling in Port Royal. Their unofficial leader was Edward Mansfield, and soon a dozen privateer ships were being made ready for sea.

On Sunday, 21 January 1663, Myngs's *Centurion* and Captain Smart's *Griffin* led this squadron out past Gallows Point, with a total of more than 1,400 men aboard. Veering westward, Myngs quickly rounded Yucatán and worked his way down past the treacherous uncharted shoals of the Gulf of Mexico, it being his intention to fall upon the slumbering tropical port of Campeche. During this passage he lost contact with his consort

This was agreed to and as a token of good faith, Myngs released all but six of his most important hostages before watering.

On the 23rd his fleet got under way, carrying off great booty and fourteen vessels found in the harbour, which were described by a Spanish eye-witness as 'three of 300 tons, the rest medium or small, and some with valuable cargo still on board'. This heavily laden formation beat its way back around Yucatán against contrary winds and currents, so laboriously that people on Jamaica began to despair as to its fate. Finally *Centurion* reached Port Royal on 23 April 1663 under the command of flag-captain Thomas Morgan, being followed 'soon after [by] the rest of the fleet, but straggling, because coming from leeward every one made the best of his way'. Despite this victory, Myngs's wounds proved so serious that he required lengthy convalescence, and early that July *Centurion* sailed for England.

His withdrawal left the West Indian freebooters without their best natural leader, so they soon began operating on their own account, in smaller individual bands. These lesser depredations continued unabated even after a new Governor, Sir Thomas Modyford, reached Jamaica in June 1664 and proclaimed 'that for the future all acts of hostility against the Spaniards should cease', as the British Crown had meanwhile negotiated better terms with Madrid and now wished to promote a more benign trade policy with regard to Spanish America. But Jamaica's buccaneers and their foreign counterparts sneered at such restrictions, brazenly violating them whenever any local friction chanced to flare up throughout that region. 'What compliance can be expected from men so desperate and numerous,' a local slaver lamented that year, 'that have no element but the sea, nor trade but privateering?'

Modyford began his rule by impounding two rich Spanish prizes brought in by the veteran captain Robert Searle, further directing that his commission 'be taken from him and his rudder and sails taken ashore for security'. But soon, circumstances began forcing the Governor to communicate privately to London that the buccaneers must be allowed to dispose of their captures on his island, as 'otherwise they will be alarmed and go to the French at Tortuga, and His Majesty will lose 1,000 or 1,500 stout men', leaving that British colony defenceless and without any significant maritime traffic. Modyford added that these renegades might even be tempted to begin attacking shipping bound for Jamaica itself, as one Captain Munro had already done, 'for they are desperate people, the greater part having been men of war for twenty years'.

In light of this seeming equivocation, adventurers such as young Morgan – despite being a militia officer, and nephew to the island's new Lieutenant-Governor, Colonel Edward Morgan – felt no compunctions about aligning themselves with rovers such as John Morris and Dutch-born David Martien, to make an unauthorised descent on the Mexican coast. These hard-bitten captains would later argue – utterly disingenuously – that 'having been out 22 months [*i.e.*, since participating in Myngs's sack of Campeche in early 1663],' they had not known of the cessation of hostilities against the Spaniards, and so continued operating under their two-and-a-half-year-old commissions from Lord Windsor.

Together they mustered a few vessels and two hundred men, departing Jamaica in January 1665 to round Yucatán. Probing cautiously down the Gulf coast, they arrived opposite Campeche one night in mid-February, where they cut out an 8-gun Spanish frigate from the roads. They then sailed

past the Laguna de Términos, coming to anchor on 19 February before the tiny town of Santa María de la Frontera, at the mouth of the Grijalva river. Some 110–120 buccaneers disembarked and travelled fifty miles upriver through its marshy channels, until the provincial capital of Villahermosa de Tabasco came into sight. At 4 o'clock on the morning of the 24th they crept into this sleeping city, capturing most of its inhabitants in their beds. A general sack ensued, after which booty and captives were loaded aboard a coaster lying in its river. The raiders then paused at nearby Santa Teresa ranch to release their women captives, retaining only the men for whom they demanded a ransom of three hundred head of cattle. Farther down the river they came upon a second coaster loaded with a valuable cargo of flour, which they also seized.

But upon regaining the river mouth, the raiders discovered their waiting ships had been captured during their absence by a Spanish naval patrol, leaving them without a means of escape from New Spain. Three Spanish frigates and 270 men had been sent out by Campeche's Lieutenant-Governor in search of the prize taken from that port, and these had sighted the interlopers' trio of vessels anchored off Santa María de la Frontera on 22 February. The British anchor-watches had fled aboard a single vessel, abandoning their 10-gun flagship and 8-gun prize, together with seven comrades. The latter had revealed to their captors that the ships had been left unmanned because 'Captain Mauricio [*sic*; Morris] and David Martin [*sic*; Martien]' had led the bulk of the rovers inland.

Their retreat cut off, the main body of freebooters released their remaining hostages and began moving westward with their two coasters, hoping to find another means of escaping back out to sea. On the

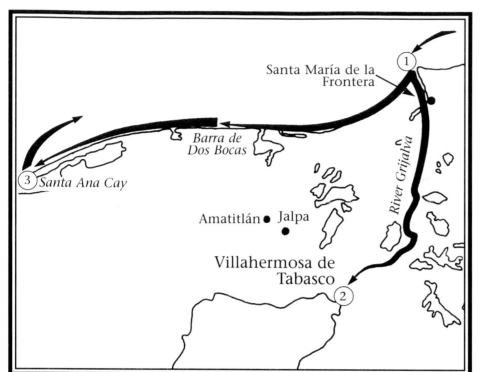

Left: Morris, Martien and Morgan's Tabasco Raid (February 1665): Having taken a prize at Campeche, the marauders then anchored opposite the bar of Tabasco (1), sending a boat party fifty miles up the Grijalva River to surprise its provincial capital of Villahermosa (2). This accomplished, they retraced their course, only to discover that their anchored ships had been captured during their absence. Retreating westward, the freebooters were overtaken at Santa Ana cay by a Spanish force (3), but succeeded in defeating these pursuers before standing out to sea.

Below: Reconstruction plan of the harbour castle at Santiago de Cuba. Following Myngs's devastating assault, it took the Spaniards several decades to rebuild this critical redoubt. (Archivo General de la Nación, Mexico).

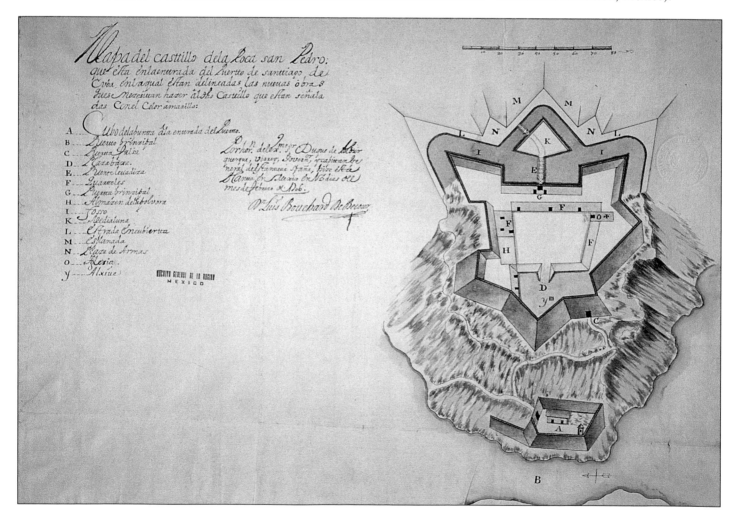

afternoon of 17 March they were overtaken by another Spanish naval patrol opposite Santa Ana cay, this time sailing the privateers' former 10-gun flagship and 8-gun prize, which the Spaniards had hastily crewed with three hundred volunteer militia from Campeche. José Aldana, the Spanish commander, sent a messenger in a boat to call upon the buccaneers to surrender, but these pretended not to understand.

When an interpreter approached shore the following morning to repeat this hail, Morris, Martien and Morgan replied they would not give up without a fight, and the Spaniards reluctantly disembarked. They discovered that the raiders had used the interval to entrench themselves behind a sturdy palisade reinforced with sandbags, and bristling with seven small cannon brought from Villahermosa. The Spanish force, comprised mostly of lightly armed citizen-soldiers, showed little stomach for an all-out assault, being easily repelled without having inflicted a single casualty among the freebooters. The next day, 19 March, the Spanish ships were found conveniently run aground, thus allowing the raiders to exit undisturbed in their two coasters.

Morris, Martien and Morgan then proceeded north-eastwards, hugging the Yucatán coastline and capturing more seaworthy boats, while

Right: Morris, Martien and Morgan's Granada Campaign (June 1665):
After capturing a Spanish ship at Trujillo (Honduras) and obtaining native guides from Cape Gracias a Dios, the rovers proceeded to Monkey Point (1) and concealed their vessels. They ascended the San Juan River in boats and traversed the Lago de Nicaragua by nocturnal stages, falling upon the unsuspecting city of Granada (2). Upon withdrawing, they plundered the island of Solentiname (3) before regaining their anchored ships, then sailed away for Jamaica (4).

making occasional disembarkations to obtain supplies. Off Sisal they looted a vessel laden with corn, whose crew they allegedly released with a message directed to the Spanish Governor, vowing to return and lay waste his province. They then rounded Yucatán and traversed the Bay of Honduras as far as Roatan, where they paused to take on water. Striking next at Trujillo, on the north coast of Honduras, they overran this port and seized a ship lying in its roads, which permitted them to press on to Cape Gracias a Dios on the Mosquito Coast. Nine native guides were hired, and these sailed with the buccaneers even further southward to Monkey Point (today Punta Mono, Nicaragua), where the vessels were hidden before the rovers headed up the San Juan River in lighter boats.

More than one hundred miles and three waterfalls later, they emerged into the great Lake of Nicaragua, crossing it by nocturnal stages and so managing to surprise the city of Granada. The buccaneers

took this place on 29 June 1665, when they:

> ... marched undescried into the centre of the city, fired a volley, overturned 18 great guns in the Plaza de Armas, took the *sargento mayor* [garrison commander's] house wherein were all their arms and ammunition, secured in the great church 300 of the best men prisoners, abundance of which were churchmen, plundered for 16 hours, discharged all the prisoners, sunk all the boats [to prevent pursuit], and so came away.

Retracing their course across the lake, at the south-eastern extremity 'they took a vessel of 100 tons and an island as large as Barbados, called Lida [*sic*; Solentiname?], which they plundered'. Amazingly, the raiders then regained their anchored vessels and by the end of August were back at Port Royal, having travelled almost three thousand miles in

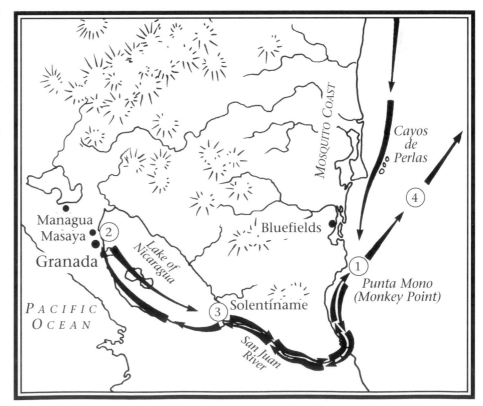

seven months, assaulting five Spanish towns and undertaking countless lesser engagements. A disapproving island merchant was moved to write: 'Although there had been peace with the Spaniards not long since proclaimed, yet the privateers went out and in, as if there had been an actual war without commission.'

The renegades knew that their transgressions would go unpunished, however, because during this rampage, trade rivalries between England and The Netherlands had become so intense that the Second Anglo–Dutch War had exploded back in Europe. (For this reason Martien did not re-enter Port Royal with the others, because 'being a Dutchman and fearing his enter-

tainment at Jamaica', he had instead sailed directly to the French *boucanier* stronghold of Tortuga Island.) But the remaining raiders realised that they would find Modyford in a forgiving mood, willing to turn a blind eye as he now needed to recruit as many privateers as possible for action against the powerful Dutch presence in the West Indies.

Indeed, Morgan's uncle had sailed four months earlier, leading just such an expedition of nine freebooter vessels and more than five hundred men against the Dutch islands of Sint Eustatius, Sabá, Curaçao and Bonaire. After a long upwind beat, the colonel had appeared off the former place, storming its beaches with 350 buccaneers. Sint Eustatius was easily

overrun, but in the words of his second in command: 'The good old colonel, leaping out of the boat and being a corpulent man, got a strain, and his spirit being great he pursued over-earnestly the enemy on a hot day, so that he surfeited and suddenly died.' The dead colonel's followers soon fell out among themselves over the division of spoils, leaving Thomas Morgan (no relation to either the colonel or his nephew Henry) in possession of that Dutch colony, while the rest of the freebooters dispersed on other pursuits.

Truth be told, England's rovers showed scant enthusiasm for campaigns against the Dutch, preferring to attack their traditional Spanish foe – notwithstanding the fact that

Left: Shore party from a Spanish plate fleet being ambushed on a West Indian isle by Caribs.

this latter country remained strictly neutral in the conflict. Finally their actions became so obnoxious that Modyford was obliged to recall his scattered forces to a rendezvous in November 1665 at Bluefields Bay, off the south-western shores of Jamaica, where he hoped to remind them of their duty. Eventually six hundred buccaneers answered his summons, responding to the Governor's call for a renewed effort against the Dutch by assuring him they were 'very forward to suppression of that enemy', and even accepting instruction for a descent against Curaçao. But as soon as Jamaica fell below the horizon, the freebooters forgot all about their promise and laid a course for the south coast of Cuba, supposedly to purchase provisions for their forthcoming campaign.

A hapless Spanish bark was intercepted among the Cayos and its 22 crew-members were murdered, after which the rovers reached the tiny port of Júcaro at about Christmas time. There their demand of 'victuals for their money' was allegedly refused, furnishing the excuse for 200–300 men who:

> ... marched 42 miles into the country, took and fired the town of Sancti Spíritus, routed a body of 200 horse, carried their prisoners to their ships, and for their ransom had 300 fat beeves [*sic*; beef-cattle] sent down [to the coast].

The raiders later justified this rapacious visit by saying that some among their number held ancient Portuguese commissions (issued by the French Governor of Tortuga), which supposedly permitted such digressions.

Having thus disposed of their supply problem, the privateers then elected Edward Mansfield their admiral, and in mid-January 1666 reassured an emissary from the Jamaican Governor that they now 'had much zeal to His Majesty's service and a firm resolution to attack Curaçao'. But this, too, quickly evaporated once they began the long upwind haul towards that island, until eventually even Mansfield's own crew refused to go any farther, 'averring publicly that there was more profit with less hazard to be gotten against the Spaniard, which was their only interest'. Consequently Mansfield fell away to leeward, steering his ships to the popular buccaneer haunt called Bocas del Toro (literally 'Bull's Mouths' or 'Entrances of the Bull', on the north-western shores of the present-day Panamanian Republic). There a fleet of fifteen privateer vessels gathered, eight sailing eastward to make a descent on the town of Natá in the Panamanian province of Veragua, while Mansfield led the remaining seven westward toward Costa Rica.

Arriving off Portete on 8 April 1666, Mansfield's contingent was able to capture that town's coastal lookout before any alarm could be sent inland, then anchored his ships off Punta del Toro. It was the Englishman's intent to take the provincial capital of Cartago by a surprise overland march, and he commenced his enterprise well by bursting upon the nearby town of Matina at the head of several hundred men, snapping up all its 35 Spanish citizens. But a lone Indian managed to escape from the smaller hamlet of Teotique, carrying word of this invasion to the Costa Rican Governor Juan López de Flor. By 15 April hundreds of Spanish militiamen had begun mustering at the mountain stronghold of Turrialba, ready to dispute the invaders' passage.

Meanwhile Mansfield was experiencing great hardships in the jungle, his men succumbing to hunger, disease and fatigue. When they encountered some natives bearing bags of ground wheat, the buccaneers fell to fighting among themselves over this meagre prize. Governor López, heartened by this report of the invaders' sagging morale, advanced with his own troops and forced Mansfield to retreat. By 23 April his survivors had staggered back aboard their ships at Portete, 'exhausted and dying of hunger', then shortly thereafter retired for Bocas del Toro. Here another two ships deserted Mansfield, leaving him in the unenviable position of being regarded as a failure both by his mercurial buccaneers, as well as by the Crown authorities on Jamaica. In a desperate effort to vindicate himself, Mansfield decided to attack the tiny Spanish garrison on the island of Providencia, which had belonged to the British more than twenty years earlier.

His two remaining frigates and three sloops raised this island at noon on 25 May 1666, gliding down toward its northern coast that evening, and dropping anchor unobserved at 10 o'clock. At about midnight the moon rose, and two hundred buccaneers rowed in through the reefs by its faint glow: more than one hundred were British, the rest being eighty Frenchmen from Tortuga, plus a few Dutch and Portuguese. These marched across the island, rounding up isolated Spanish residents, then stormed the lone citadel at first light on the 26th, without suffering a single loss. Only eight Spanish soldiers were found asleep inside, the remaining 62 being scattered among their civilian billets. Mansfield granted all the inhabitants quarter, and the French *flibustiers* prevented the British from ransacking the church.

Ten days later Mansfield set sail again with 170 Spanish captives whom he had promised to restore to their compatriots. Captain Hatsell was left in command of the island with 35 privateers and fifty black slaves, until the admiral or some other British official returned. On 11 June 1666 Mansfield touched at Punta de Brujas ('Witches Point') on the north coast of Panama, where he deposited his prisoners before standing away for Jamaica. On 22 June he arrived with just two ships at Port Royal, where he encountered a piece of good fortune: for three and a half months previously, Modyford and the Council had resolved 'that it is the interest and advantage of the island of Jamaica to have letters of marque granted against the Spaniard', despite the peaceful relations with that nation on the far side of the Atlantic.

The Governor had justified his unilateral decision to authorise these depredations by complaining of the local Spaniards' continuing hostility, claiming: 'it must be force alone that can cut in sunder that unneighbourly maxim of their government to deny all access of strangers'. Aside from this constant friction, Modyford had further become convinced that Jamaica's economy depended upon the profits from this low-grade buccaneering warfare; thus although Mansfield had not been commissioned to attack anyone except the Dutch, he now found his seizure of Providencia retroactively approved. 'I have yet only reproved him for doing it without order,' Modyford explained rather lamely to the

British Secretary of State four days later, 'which I should suppose would have been an acceptable service had he received command for it.'

The war in Europe had also taken yet another surprising twist, when it was learned that France had joined Holland against England earlier that spring. By April 1666 this news had reached the Leeward Islands, where the British immediately responded by concentrating their strength around the island of Saint Christopher (St Kitts), hoping to wrest it in its entirety from the French settlers with whom they shared it. In the forefront of these British mercenaries figured Thomas Morgan's 260 tough Jamaican buccaneers, who had been occupying Dutch Sint

Eustatius ever since Colonel Edward Morgan's sudden death from heat-stroke, and who now hastened over in seven boats to participate in this latest round of fighting.

When the French settlers of Saint Christopher attacked first, at dawn on 22 April, the local British Governor, William Watts – clad only in his night-gown and slippers – had attempted to instruct Morgan to lead the main body of British forces against the smaller enemy concentration remaining at their stronghold of Pointe de Sable, while he himself took a company and looted the Frenchmen's plantations during their absence. Incensed at this self-serving proposal, the hard-bitten Morgan poked his loaded pistol into Watts's chest, called him a coward, and threatened to shoot if he did not immediately order both units to advance into battle.

Thus persuaded, Watts hastily dressed and led the main British army of 1,400 men against the French positions, with Morgan's buccaneers marching in the van. This host crested a hill shortly before noon on the 22nd and gazed down upon the French defences of Pointe de Sable, which were being held by a mere 350 men under Robert Lonvilliers de Poincy. Confident of victory, Watts and Morgan brought their army down through the surrounding cane-fields, which were soon set ablaze in fires and counter-fires by scouts from both sides. Amid this smoke and confusion, Morgan drove directly toward the French centre, but Lonvilliers countered by placing the musketeers of Bernard Lafond de l'Esperance in ambush behind a hedge of brushwood. Morgan's first attack was halted in its tracks by a deadly volley, after which his buccaneers

Left: Contemporary depiction of the murderous battle fought between French and English buccaneers at Pointe de Sable, on the West Indian island of St Kitts, in April 1666.

gamely rallied, going in for a second assault.

A brutal half-hour of gunplay ensued, in which marksmen on both sides encountered opponents as skilful and well-armed as themselves. The ensuing slaughter was horrific, but finally the buccaneers fought their way through, emerging from the hedge to come into contact with the French main body, where they fatally wounded Lonvilliers. But as another group of Jamaicans advanced against Lafond's stronghold, they found the French had mounted a cannon on a farm wagon, loaded to the muzzle with grapeshot. When the buccaneers swarmed in close, a single blast decimated their ranks, and blew away the last shreds of their courage. Morgan fell badly wounded, being borne from the blood-drenched field by his men. Of the 260 who had plunged into this ferocious firefight, only seventeen emerged unhurt.

Seeing the buccaneers falter, Watts circled warily round the French positions with his staff and some soldiers, hoping to find a better line of advance for his own main force. But the sharp-eyed Lafond spotted this movement, and again stationed a company of musketeers in ambush. The British Governor wandered too close to their hiding-place, and a single volley dropped him and most of his retinue. Thus his militiamen were left leaderless, blazing away ineffectively at the enemy defences from long range over the next two hours, until they finally began to run low on powder and withdrew. Demoralised, the British survivors retreated to a fort on their own half of the island, which they then precipitously abandoned, after having spiked its guns. The units then collapsed into total chaos, even pillaging Watts's home in Old Road Town, before Lafond's columns arrived overland to consummate the French conquest of Saint Christopher.

British fortunes in this region were dealt a further heavy blow when Lord Willoughby, Governor of the Windward Islands, led an ill-fated relief expedition from Barbados three months later. His eighteen small vessels and more than one thousand men were engulfed by a hurricane somewhere between Guadeloupe and the Saintes, starting at 6 o'clock on the evening of 4 August 1666, which ended with almost all of them being wholly destroyed. Thus when a small French squadron under Lefebvre de la Barre reached Martinique on 1 October, followed by a Dutch one under Abraham Crijnssen which touched at Suriname in February 1667, these gave the two continental allies naval superiority in the Caribbean. It was not until London rushed out reinforcements under Captain John Berry and Rear-Admiral Sir John Harman a few months later, that this Franco–Dutch combination could be directly challenged, by which time numerous British outposts had already been captured and enemy corsairs given free rein.

Perhaps the most notorious of the latter proved to be Jean-David Nau, nicknamed 'l'Olonnais' because he was originally from the port of Les Sables-d'Olonne in the Vendée, France. Nau had reputedly arrived at Saint-Domingue many years before as an *engagé* or indentured servant, from which he rose to become one of the sharpshooting hunters known as *boucaniers*, then later a sea-rover or *flibustier*. His earliest campaigns had included cruises against both Cuba and Campeche, where he had once been shipwrecked, although managing to escape. Like his British contemporaries, Nau showed a marked propensity for attacking the local Spanish–Americans rather than his country's official enemies, in no small part because of his great personal animosity against them. By early 1667 his reputation was such that he was able to muster a large

Sailing into the Gulf of Venezuela, Nau disembarked his *flibustiers* near the battery guarding the Bar of Maracaibo, which consisted 'of sixteen cannon surrounded by several gabions or earth-filled wicker cylinders, with a ramp of earth thrown against them to shelter the men inside'. His *boucaniers* quickly overran this feeble fortification, and passed their ships over the Bar into the Laguna. Next day they reached Maracaibo, which they found abandoned, and occupied it for the next two weeks. During this period buccaneer patrols were sent out into the outlying areas to bring in prisoners, a few being tortured by Nau himself to reveal their riches, with little result. Consequently he crossed the Laguna to the south-eastern town of Gibraltar (near present-day Bobures), which the Spaniards had reinforced with several hundred troops. Nonplussed, Nau's *flibustiers* roared into battle and Gibraltar fell after a fierce struggle, in which forty buccaneers were killed and thirty wounded.

The Spaniards suffered much heavier casualties, hundreds of their bodies being loaded on to two old boats to be towed a mile out into the Laguna and sunk. The town was then ruthlessly pillaged over the next month, after which Nau demanded a ransom of ten thousand pesos from the interior, to leave its buildings intact. Once this was paid, he and his *flibustiers* recrossed the Laguna and extorted a ransom of twenty thousand pesos and five hundred head of cattle to spare Maracaibo as well. Two

force of *flibustiers* for a major expedition.

He quit Tortuga at the end of April 1667 with a flotilla of eight small vessels and 660 men, pausing at Bayahá on the north coast of Hispaniola for an additional party of *boucaniers* and a large stock of provisions. He ignored the heavy fighting which was raging throughout the Lesser Antilles that spring between various French, Dutch and British formations, but three months later learned of news that was much more to his liking: a new diplomatic rupture had occurred between France and Spain.

Finding this latter opponent infinitely more palatable, Nau immediately probed into the nearby Mona Passage, where he sighted a 16-gun Spanish vessel, which had just departed Puerto Rico, and gave chase. The Spaniard struck to Nau's 10-gun sloop 'after two or three hours' combat', proving to be bound for Veracruz with a rich consignment of cacao. Nau sent this vessel back to Tortuga to unload, meanwhile taking up station with the rest of his flotilla off Saona Island. While waiting for his first prize to return, Nau took a second, an 8-gun Spanish ship carrying gunpowder and *situados* (payrolls) for the garrisons of Santo Domingo and Cumaná. When his first prize rejoined, Nau made it his flagship and felt sufficiently strengthened to attempt a full-scale descent against the Spanish Main, which he had combed that previous year.

months after he had penetrated it, Nau finally quit the Laguna entirely, and eight days later touched at Île-à-Vache to divide his plunder. Shortly thereafter he visited Jamaica – peace having since been restored with England via the Treaty of Breda – and sold off an 80-ton, 12-gun Spanish brigantine to yet another infamous raider of that age: the Dutch-born Rok Brasiliano. One month later, Nau regained Tortuga Island and was given a hero's welcome.

Some time later, he sortied again with seven hundred *flibustiers*, three hundred of them aboard his new flagship, the largest Spanish prize he had carried away from

Above: Contemporary portrait of Jean-David (or perhaps Jean-David-François) Nau, more commonly known as l'Olonnais.

Right: Alleged cruelty of l'Olonnais. In this lurid depiction, the *flibustier* chieftain tears the heart out of a Honduran captive and force-feeds it to another, during his march upon San Pedro Sula. While doubtless brutal, the practical difficulties of Nau's atrocity makes this story seem highly apocryphal.

Tillac inv. et del.

66 Jean David François Nau en 1666 dit l'Olonnois, et Michel le Basque, généraux des aventuriers français de la Tortue dans l'expédition contre Maracaibo.

Left: Modern depiction of Michel le Basque (left) and Nau l'Olonnais during their Maracaibo campaign, by Pablo Tillac.

Right: Mexican aristocrat and his lady, c. 1650. In the absence of royal regiments stationed in the New World, Spain's empire had to be defended by *hidalgo* militiamen. While brave, these proved indifferent campaigners, especially against the elusive, more heavily-armed buccaneers. (Museo de América, Madrid)

Maracaibo. In company with five lesser craft, Nau proceeded to Bayahá once more, to take on 'salt meat for their victuals', after which he cruised southern Cuba as far as the Gulf of Batabanó, seizing boats to use in his next project: an ascent of the San Juan river. Evidently Nau hoped to emulate Morris, Martien and Morgan's feat of three years previously by sacking Granada, but when he attempted to clear Cape Gracias a Dios and steer southward, his cumbersome

new flagship was prevented by a lack of wind, and instead drifted westward along the north shores of Honduras. Running low on provisions, Nau was obliged to dispatch foraging parties up the Aguán river, and eventually was driven as far west as Puerto Cabellos.

Here he captured a Spanish merchantman armed with 24 cannon and sixteen *pedreros* or swivel-guns, as well as occupying that town. He terrified two captives into leading him inland against San Pedro Sula,

the nearest city, setting off with three hundred *flibustiers* while his Dutch lieutenant Mozes van Klijn garrisoned the tiny port. Less than ten miles into the jungle Nau's men were waylaid by a party of Spaniards, and learned from prisoners that more ambushes had been prepared deeper inland. Furious, Nau instructed his men to give no quarter, for he believed in the old pirate practice of minimising resistance by sowing terror among his prey. Despite this, the Spaniards sprang more ambushes and even fought off Nau's initial assault on San Pedro Sula, being allowed to evacuate under a flag of truce. The city and its outlying region were then pillaged over the next few days, and burnt to the ground when Nau retired to the coast.

Upon returning to Puerto Cabellos, he learned that a rich galleon was due to arrive soon from Spain 'at the Guatemala river' (*i.e.*, the Bay of Amatique), and so posted a pair of lookout boats off its southern shores, while leading the rest of his vessels across to the western side of the Gulf of Honduras to careen. Three months of idleness ensued, until word was finally received that the galleon had arrived. Recalling his scattered forces, Nau quickly attacked, although the Spaniard mounted 42 cannon and had a crew of 130 men.

Right: Rok Brasiliano, a Dutch-born rover who operated out of Jamaica. Having purchased a Spanish prize from l'Olonnais, he later served under Morgan at both Portobelo and Panama.

His own 28-gun flagship and a smaller buccaneer consort were beaten off, but four boatloads of *flibustiers* carried the galleon by storming its bulwarks. The booty proved to be most disappointing, however, as the bulk of its cargo had already been unloaded and sent inland, there remaining only some iron, paper and wine.

As quickly as Nau's star had risen, it now began to plummet. Discouraged, his confederates Van Klijn and Pierre le Picard decided to quit his company, leaving him alone with his Maracaibo prize. This was such a heavy sailer, that a short time later it ran aground among the Cayos de Perlas (near present-day Bluefields, Nicaragua). Nau and his crew were forced to live ashore, planting crops and attempting to build a longboat from their vessel's remains. When this was finally completed five or six months later, it was not big enough to accommodate all the survivors, so Nau went with a group of men to the mouth of the San Juan river, hoping to steal more boats and return for the others.

But instead he was defeated by the Spaniards and forced to flee even farther away, sailing into the Gulf of Darien in a desperate bid to obtain more craft. Here his small band was at last set upon by the local natives, and according to its sole survivor, 'l'Olonnais was hacked to pieces and roasted limb by limb'. In the harsh world of the pirate, a similar fate would await many.

Right: Dutch view of the harbour at San Juan, Puerto Rico. Although the ships are accurately rendered, this scene is otherwise fictitious.

PORTO RICO

IV

Harry Morgan's Way

Standing upon the margent of the Main,
Whilst the high boiling tide came tumbling in,
I felt my fluctuating thoughts maintain
As great an ocean, and as rude, within.
Charles Cotton (1630–87)

Left: Portrait of a teenage Henry Morgan, presumably painted shortly before his departure for Jamaica.

With peace restored against Holland, and an Anglo–French entente gradually emerging against Spain, the stage was now set for a colourful new leader to unite all West Indian privateers. Henry Morgan had been born either in Penkarne or nearby Llanrhymny (present-day Rhymney), Wales, the son of a military family. His uncles had both served as professional soldiers of fortune on the continent during the Thirty Years War, then later achieved high rank in the English Civil War, on either side of that conflict. Morgan himself had grown up into this martial tradition as well, although too young to have participated in any of these early hostilities. Years later he would confess that he had left school at too early an age to receive much formal education, having 'been more used to the pike than the book'.

Upon turning nineteen years of age, he apparently embarked as a subaltern in Oliver Cromwell's 'Western Design', sailing under Admiral Penn and General Venables in the expedition that eventually conquered Jamaica. As we have seen, several years of abject misery followed for Morgan and the rest of his fellow-soldiers on that island, as thousands succumbed to tropical

Amphibious warfare in the seventeenth century: Spanish soldiers and warships (left, centre) help defend a coastal keep against a Dutch attack in Flanders. The weapons and tactics developed during the several decades of continual warfare in the Low Countries — in which so many European mercenaries, such as Morgan's uncles, came to serve — were easily transposed to the vast new battlefields of the West Indies and Spanish America. (National Maritime Museum, Greenwich)

disease, Spanish guerrilla warfare, and general neglect by the high command in London.

Such an ordeal marked its survivors, leaving them distrustful of far-distant ministers who did not seem to have their best interests at heart. The young Welshman was one of the fortunate few who survived this experience, and when the remnant of that skeletal army was reorganised into five militia units by Lord Windsor in 1662, Morgan became a captain in the Port Royal Volunteer Regiment. He also received a privateering commission for a tiny vessel lying in its roads, with which he participated in the raids against Santiago de Cuba and Campeche under Myngs, as well as Tabasco and Granada under Morris and Martien.

Following his return from this latter expedition in August 1665, Morgan married his first cousin Mary Elizabeth Morgan, who had recently come out from England with her father, Colonel Edward Morgan. As has been noted, this officer was Lieutenant-Governor of Jamaica, a position in which he proved so supportive to his superior Modyford that the latter wrote to London: 'I find the character of Colonel Morgan short of his worth and am infinitely obliged to His Majesty for sending so worthy a person to assist me, whom I really cherish as my brother.' Therefore, when news arrived that Edward Morgan had died during his attack on Dutch Sint Eustatius, his young nephew inherited this influence, and his own position rapidly began to rise. In February 1666, Morgan was promoted colonel of his militia regiment, and assigned to supervise the expansion of Port Royal's harbour defences, because of fears of an enemy invasion.

But a still more significant elevation was to occur the following year, when it was learnt that the great freebooter 'Admiral' Edward Mansfield had died. In a clever bid to settle the unofficial mantle of

buccaneer leader on to a loyal Crown officer, Modyford commissioned Morgan in late 1667 – during a period of renewed anti-Spanish fears – 'to draw together the English privateers and take prisoners of the Spanish nation, whereby he might inform of the intention of that enemy to invade Jamaica'.

Such an open-ended licence meant that rovers veritably flocked to Morgan's rendezvous off the south cays of Cuba, eager to join a man whom they regarded as a kindred spirit in officially sanctioned mischief. Among his many new

adherents was John Morris, formerly his commander during the raids against Tabasco and Granada, as well as numerous French *flibustiers* (whose own country was still legally at war with Spain, thus adding further legitimacy to this enterprise). After holding consultations with his various captains, Morgan led this formation of a dozen ships and seven hundred

Below: Morgan's men and his French allies (right) push into the streets of Puerto Príncipe (modern Camagüey, Cuba) in April 1668.

men into the Gulf of Ana María, setting a large landing party ashore on 28 March 1668 to raid the inland town of Puerto Príncipe (present-day Camagüey).

The Spaniards attempted to dispute this incursion with militia cavalry and native lancers, but these were helpless before the superior firepower of the buccaneers, who inflicted almost one hundred casu-

Below: Morgan's men storm the Santiago citadel at Portobelo, Panama, on 11 July 1668. Note the liberal use of hand grenades and scaling ladders.

alties before carrying the town by storm. Fifteen days of pillage ensued, although the freebooters withdrew with only fifty thousand pieces of eight in money, a paltry sum when redistributed among so many. None the less the Spaniards also provided several hundred head of cattle to ransom their fellow citizens who had been carried off as hostages, so that Morgan left Cuba well supplied, and headed his force towards Cape Gracias a Dios on the Central American coast.

Here the two national contingents parted company, when Mor-

gan suggested they next make a descent on the Panamanian port of Portobelo, terminus of the annual plate fleets. The French 'wholly refused to join with us in that action', Morgan later reported, evidently disappointed by the meagre purchase already obtained at Puerto Príncipe, and preferring their own independent operation. Morgan remained undiscouraged, having supposedly extracted sufficient intelligence from his Cuban captives apropos hostile designs against Jamaica, as to justify still further depredations against the Spaniards on his own.

With the four frigates, eight sloops and fewer than five hundred men left to him, Morgan sailed down the Central American coast and anchored at Bocas del Toro. Here he transferred his men into 23 *piraguas* and smaller boats, rowing 150 miles eastward in four nights, until he arrived in the vicinity of Portobelo on the afternoon of 10 July 1668. That night his flotilla disgorged its men and Morgan led them in a swift overland march, taking the stunned Spanish citizenry by surprise at daybreak. A terrified eye-witness later reported that the buccaneers fired 'off their guns at everything alive, whites, blacks, even dogs, in order to spread terror', and so secured the town without suffering a single loss.

Portobelo's eighty-man citadel held out for a couple of hours longer, until Morgan rounded up a group of captives – including the *alcalde* (mayor), two friars, several nuns and other women – who acted as a human shield for a party of buccaneers that approached the citadel's main gate bearing torches and axes. The Spanish defenders reluctantly opened fire, wounding two clerics and killing an Englishman, but were unable to prevent these sappers from reaching their gate. While thus distracted, another band of buccaneers used scaling ladders to enter unobserved on the far

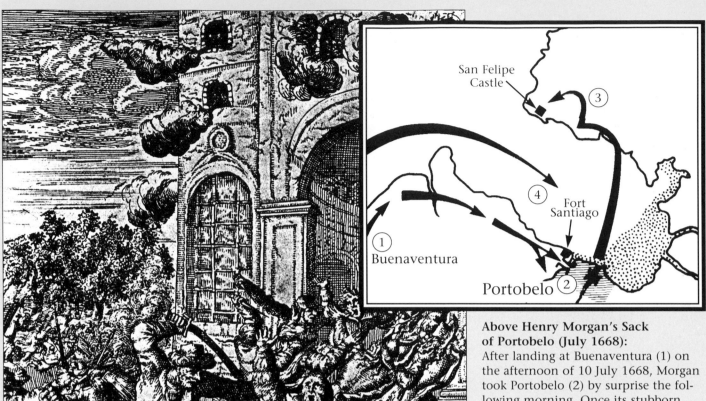

After landing at Buenaventura (1) on the afternoon of 10 July 1668, Morgan took Portobelo (2) by surprise the following morning. Once its stubborn Santiago citadel surrendered, he crossed the bay and drove the defenders out of San Felipe castle next day (3), thus allowing his ships to enter the roads (4) safely.

Tomorrow we plan to burn this city to the ground and then set sail with all the guns and munitions from the castles. With us we will take all our prisoners and we will show them the same kindness that the English prisoners have received in this place.

Above: Massacre of Portobelo's garrison after the triumph of Morgan's buccaneers. Some of the latter (left) are depicted in Moorish garb, presumably as a commentary upon their viciousness.

side of the fortress, planting 'their red flag on the castle walls', and carrying the entire building by storm. At least 45 Spanish soldiers died during this vicious bloodbath, the rest being wounded.

Next morning Morgan led two hundred buccaneers across the bay and after a token resistance, forced the surrender of the fifty Spanish soldiers still holding out in Portobelo's harbour castle. This allowed his ships to enter shortly thereafter from Bocas del Toro, so that at the cost of only eighteen buccaneers dead, the port and its defences were wholly his. Wealthy citizens were then tortured to reveal their hidden riches, and many other excesses were committed. Finally, on the 14th, Morgan wrote a letter – in good Spanish – to the President of the Audiencia of Panama, saying:

Notwithstanding this rather ominous tone, Morgan further offered to spare the city if a ransom of 350,000 pesos were paid. The Acting President of Panama, Agustín de Bracamonte, was already marching to Portobelo's relief at the head of eight hundred militiamen, and haughtily responded: 'I take you to be a corsair and I reply that the vassals of the King of Spain do not make treaties with inferior persons.'

An unabashed Morgan wrote back:

Although your letter does not deserve a reply, since you call me a corsair, nevertheless I write you these few lines to ask you to come quickly. We are waiting for you with great pleasure and we have powder and ball with which to receive you. If you do not come very soon, we will, with the favour of God and our arms, come and visit you in Panama. Now it is our intention to garrison the castles and keep them for the King of England, my master, who since he had a mind to seize them, has also a mind to keep them. And since I do not believe that you have sufficient men to fight with me tomorrow, I will order all the poor prisoners to be freed so that they may go to help you.

Much to his chagrin, Bracamonte's army proved too weak to assault Morgan's positions when he arrived outside Portobelo next day, and the Spaniards were forced to remain encamped miserably for a week in the outlying jungle. Finally, on 24 July Bracamonte ordered a full-scale retreat, leaving one of his subordinates to negotiate the ransom. This was eventually set at 100,000 pesos and paid in the first days of August, after which Morgan loaded up his ships and sailed away, returning to a hero's welcome at Port Royal on the 27th.

Less than a month and a half later (early October 1668) he was ready to return to sea, again calling on freebooters to join him at Île-à-Vache for yet another enterprise against the Spaniards. Modyford continued to support his 'admiral' in the premise that these strikes were a strategic necessity, pre-empting an enemy invasion of Jamaica. When the 34-gun frigate HMS *Oxford* reached Port Royal shortly after Morgan had sailed (having been sent out from England to perform peacetime patrol duty off that

island, at the colony's expense), Modyford decided to send it as a reinforcement for Morgan 'to face Cartagena'. The veteran privateersman Edward Collier was appointed to command *Oxford* after her Royal Naval captain killed his own sailing master in a duel at Port Morant that November, and the frigate's crew was then further fleshed out to a total of 160 men.

The new commander set sail on 20 December, with additional instructions from Modyford to detain the 14-gun French corsair *Cerf Volant* ('Kite') out of La Rochelle, which had recently plundered a Virginia merchantman. Upon arriving off Île-à-Vache, Collier found the culprit lying among Morgan's assembled flotilla, and invited the French captain aboard *Oxford*. Having been identified and denounced by the aggrieved Virginian (whom Collier was conveying aboard his ship), Capitaine Vivien and his 45-man crew were then arrested, and taken back to Port Royal in their ship for adjudication. *Cerf Volant* was quickly condemned, renamed *Satisfaction*, and incorporated back into Morgan's fleet.

On 12 January 1669 (2 January in the Old Style calendar), Morgan and his colleagues decided that since 900–1,000 freebooters had already mustered, this was sufficient strength to attempt the great port of Cartagena on the Spanish Main, after which they began a feast to celebrate both their forthcoming voyage, and the New Year. Captains Aylett, Bigford, Collier, Morris, Thornbury and Whiting all sat down to dinner with Morgan on *Oxford*'s quarter-deck, while sailors caroused in the forecastle. 'They drank the health of the King of England and toasted their good success and fired off salvoes,' a chronicler later reported, until suddenly – the magazine exploded! Ship's surgeon Richard Browne, who was sitting towards the foot of the officers'

table on the same side as Morgan, wrote: 'I was eating my dinner with the rest, when the mainmasts blew out and fell upon Captains Aylett, Bigford and others, and knocked them on the head.'

Only six men and four boys survived this accident, out of a company numbering more than two hundred. Miraculously, Morgan, Collier and Morris all survived this spectacular blast, but the loss of so many others ended any prospects for a campaign against Cartagena or any other such major strongholds.

Collier departed with *Satisfaction* to make an independent cruise against Campeche, while Morgan transferred into the 14-gun frigate *Lilly* and led his remaining forces eastward, hoping to at least raid the smaller islands of Trinidad or Margarita (off present-day Venezuela). But by the time he got to Saona Island at the eastern end of Santo Domingo, three more of his best ships had deserted, leaving him with only eight and five hundred men. (His loyal commanders were Morris, Jeffery Pennant, Edward Dempster, Richard Norman, Richard Dobson, Adam Brewster and one other.) It was then that one of Morgan's French followers suggested a repeat of Nau l'Olonnais' feat of two years earlier, by raiding the rich and vulnerable Laguna de Maracaibo.

Morgan and his remaining consorts agreed, and after touching at Aruba a few weeks later to stock up provisions, the buccaneer fleet stood into the Gulf of Venezuela. On 9 March 1669 they were nearing the Bar of Maracaibo, when they saw that it had been fortified since Nau's incursion. A small, eleven-gun castle covered the channel, so the freebooters landed and besieged its defenders. There were actually only one Spanish officer and eight soldiers within this keep, who put up a brave show of resistance before slipping out of the fort that night, leaving a long fuse burning slowly towards the magazine. Morgan and an assault column meanwhile edged nervously into the darkened fortress, 'amazed to find no defenders', until a search revealed the fuse, which was supposedly extinguished 'about an inch away from the powder' (according to the melodramatic account left by the buccaneer Alexandre-Olivier Exquemelin, who was evidently present at this affair).

After spiking the castle's guns, Morgan's ships negotiated the shoals and made for Maracaibo, which was abandoned without resistance by its terrified citizenry, despite the Spanish governor's plea that all local militiamen present themselves 'on pain of their lives as traitors to the kingdom'. But when only twelve actually reported for duty, he too took to his heels. The exultant buccaneers sent raiding parties into the surrounding countryside 'with complete liberty and no resistance'; they rounded-up scores of prisoners who were brutally tortured to reveal their riches. After three weeks, Morgan crossed to the south-eastern side of the Laguna, visiting a like treatment upon the town of Gibraltar. By 17 April he was back at Maracaibo with a captured Cuban merchant ship and five smaller *piraguas* from Gibraltar, ready to head back out into the open sea.

But while Morgan's freebooters had been ransacking the interior, Spain's naval squadron for the West Indies – the Armada de Barlovento or 'Windward Fleet' – had arrived outside the Laguna, bottling up its exit. Admiral Alonso de Campos y Espinosa had brought with him the 412-ton flagship *Magdalena* of 38 guns, the 218-ton *San Luis* of 26 guns, and 50-ton *Nuestra Señora de la Soledad* ('Our Lady of Solitude', alias *Marquesa* or 'Marchioness') of 14 guns, all manned by a total of five hundred officers, troops and sailors. Finding the fortress gutted,

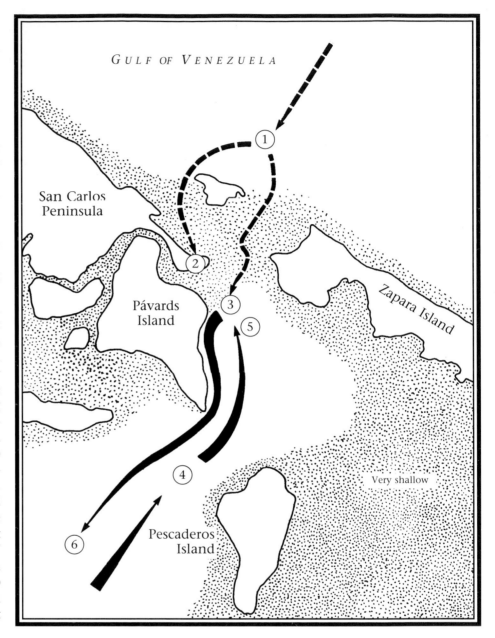

the Spanish admiral immediately reoccupied it with forty arquebusiers, repaired six of its guns, then sent messages to the inland provinces calling for further assistance. After several days he also lightened his warships and crossed these over the Bar, and when all preparations were complete, sent a letter to Morgan calling on him to surrender, because he had:

... orders to destroy you utterly and put every man to the sword. This is my final resolution: take heed, and be not

ungrateful for my kindness. I have with me valiant soldiers, yearning to be allowed to revenge the unrighteous acts you have committed against the Spanish nation in America.

When Morgan received this missive at Maracaibo, he read it aloud to his followers in the city's deserted marketplace: as one, they roared back that they would rather fight to the death than hand over their spoils, as having risked their lives for them once, they were now willing to do so again.

Opposite page: Morgan's Victory at the Bar of Maracaibo (April 1669): While Morgan's buccaneers were ransacking inland, three Spanish warships arrived outside Maracaibo's bar (1), remanned its devastated fort (2), then worked through the channel to trap the raiders inside (3). Morgan returned and confronted the Spaniards for two days (4), before finally launching a devastating strike (5). But despite having destroyed all three Spanish men o' war, he still could not get past its fort, so retired to Maracaibo (6), before returning again at a later date to slip past through guile.

Therefore, after a week spent priming for battle, Morgan's thirteen vessels approached the Bar, coming within sight of the anchored Spaniards on 25 April 1669. Two days later they suddenly darted towards the Armada at nine o'clock in the morning, led by their large Cuban prize, flying an admiral's regalia. This craft bore down menacingly upon Campos's flagship, and grappled; but when the Spanish soldiery swarmed over its bulwarks in a counter-assault, they found its decks lined only with wooden dummies, and a party of twelve buccaneers decamping hastily over the far side. The Spaniards had been cleverly duped, for the Cuban ship unexpectedly erupted into flames, and *Magdalena* soon became engulfed, forcing Campos and his panic-stricken men to leap into the water.

Seeing this terrible spectacle of their flagship being consumed right down to the waterline, the smaller *San Luis* and *Marquesa* cut their cables and ran for the shelter of the fort's guns, pursued by an angry swarm of buccaneer craft. The pair of Spanish warships ran aground in the shallows and were deliberately set ablaze by their crews in order to prevent capture, although the latter vessel was so quickly boarded that its flames were extinguished by the buccaneers, who then refloated it and incoporated it into their flotilla.

But notwithstanding this stunning victory, Morgan could still not get past the fort guarding the Bar. Its garrison had been further reinforced by seventy militiamen from the interior, as well as most of the Armada sailors who had managed to struggle ashore. When Morgan attempted a land assault that next day, this was easily beaten off, and his ships retired to Maracaibo. From there he sent the Spanish commander a proposal for a ceasefire and safe passage back out to sea for his buccaneers, in exchange for the captives they held, but this was refused. The impasse was finally broken when Morgan struck upon a second cunning scheme: for having

Below: Morgan's victory at the bar of Maracaibo, 27 April 1669. The 38-gun Spanish flagship *Magdalena* (right foreground) explodes after being set ablaze by a fireship, while the 26-gun *San Luis* (centre background) burns down to its waterline, and 14-gun *Marquesa* is captured (right background).

learnt that only half the fort's guns were actually functional, he knew he had found his way.

Returning to the Bar a few days later, his boats began busily plying back and forth in toward shore that afternoon, seemingly depositing a large contingent out of sight of the fortress, behind a screen of trees. The Spaniards, who had warily observed this activity from a distance, manhandled their six guns into the landward embrasures and braced for a nocturnal assault. But Morgan had again deceived them, his crowded boats merely hiding men in their bottoms during their return trips to the ships, so that no men had actually disembarked. Under cover of darkness, his vessels instead silently weighed and slipped past the fortress on the land breeze, whilst its defenders spent a sleepless night anticipating a ferocious assault from his phantom army.

The truth only dawned the following morn, when they beheld the buccaneer ships depositing their prisoners outside the Bar, before sailing off amid derisive hoots and jeers.

By 27 May 1669 Morgan was once more back at Port Royal, this time apparently destined to retire from roving. During his absence Secretary of State Lord Arlington had again reiterated the Crown's objections to such anti-Spanish hostilities, which Modyford felt compelled to proclaim publicly throughout Jamaica on June 24th, adding that he had further been instructed 'that the subjects of His Catholic Majesty be from now until further order treated and used as good neighbours and friends.' Such a direct command might have at least curtailed some of the more flagrant violations of the peace, were it not for the fact that in the interim

Above: Spanish men-of-war at Maracaibo's bar.

Madrid had also implemented a much more bellicose policy of its own.

On April 20th of that same year, the Queen Regent of Spain, Mariana, had authorized the issuance of privateering commissions throughout the Americas against English vessels, as a direct retaliation for Morgan's sack of Portobelo. But the cumbersome Spanish imperial bureaucracy did not actually begin granting these licenses in the New World until several months later, during which time there had been a number of arrests and detentions made by the English authorities, and a steady decline to their depredations. Hence when the first Spanish American permits began to circulate in early 1670, followed soon after by an escalation in hostile acts against English ships, these would be misconstrued on Jamaica and other West Indian islands as a deliberate breach of faith by the treacherous Spaniards.

By far and away the most annoying of this new wave of Spanish corsairs would be Manoel Rivero Pardal, a swaggering Portuguese-born mercenary who received his commission from the Governor of Cartagena on 3 January 1670, then set sail from that port three days afterwards, with a crew of seventy desperados aboard his ship *San Pedro* (more commonly called the *Fama*). It was his intention to first make a raid on Point Morant, Jamaica, to scoop up a large number of slaves, but unfavourable winds carried him past his chosen target to the Cayman Islands. Frustrated in his original design, Rivero therefore vented his wrath by burning down half the English fishermen's shacks on Grand Cayman, then took a ketch, a canoe and four children captives, which he carried off to Cuba.

Upon arriving at that island he learned of an even more tempting target: an English privateering vessel lying in the roads at Manzanillo, the port for the inland town of Bayamo. This was the *Mary and Jane*, a small ship commanded by an old Dutch rover who had settled on Jamaica, called Bernard Claesen Speirdyke (known affectionately as 'Captain Bart' to his English friends). Ironically, Speirdyke had been despatched under a flag of truce to convey letters from Modyford to the local Cuban authorities 'signifying peace between the two nations,' and restore some Spanish prisoners to their compatriots. This humanitarian work done, Speirdyke then discreetly sold off his contraband cargo among the people of Manzanillo, before standing out towards sea. Just as *Mary and Jane* was quitting the bay, he saw a ship flying English colours which hailed and asked whence he came. 'From Jamaica,' Speirdyke replied.

'Defend yourself, dog!' Rivero shouted back. 'I come as a punishment for heretics!' *Fama* opened fire, and a brisk cannonade ensued between the two until dark. The following day the Spanish vessel closed to board, *Mary and Jane* being heavily outnumbered, with only eighteen men in its crew. Despite such heavy odds, a staunch resistance was made, in which fully a third of Rivero's men were killed or incapacitated before Speirdyke's ship could be subdued. Five of the *Mary and Jane*'s crew lay dead, including its brave Dutch captain – that 'obstinate, mad heretic,' as Rivero labelled him. The victorious corsair then sent nine prisoners

Left:: Typical Dutch privateer captain.

back to Port Royal in their boat, with an inflammatory document declaring that 'he had letters of reprisal from the King of Spain for five years through the whole West Indies, for satisfaction of the Jamaicans taking Portobelo.'

While this provocative statement was being conveyed to the English, Rivero sailed his prize back to Cartagena, arriving there on 23 March 1670. A grand fiesta was held to celebrate his triumph, the first the Spaniards had been able to hold in many a long while; and because of these heady accolades, others stepped forward to emulate his example. Scarcely a month later, two more corsair vessels lay fitting out in Cartagena's roads, with Rivero flying a royal standard as 'admiral' to this motley force.

Meanwhile an ugly reaction was brewing on Jamaica, where news of the popular Speirdyke's death had been followed by rumours of yet other Spanish aggressions. These were confirmed by a copy of another Spaniard's commission, relayed to Modyford by the friendly Dutch Governor of Curaçao: it had been issued at Santiago de Cuba to one Francisco Galesio on 5 February 1670, authorizing him – like his fellow Spanish privateers – to 'proceed against the English in the Indies with every sort of hostility.' Anger swept through Jamaica upon reading these words, and Modyford was hard pressed to prevent an immediate retaliatory strike by his cantankerous buccaneers.

Here matters might have remained, but for the fact that at the end of May 1670 Rivero again sortied from Cartagena, accompanied by the *Gallardina* [a former French *flibustier* vessel, seized by the Spaniards two years earlier]. In a second deliberately provocative act, these appeared off Jamaica on June 11th, flying English colours. They pursued the merchant sloop of William Harris for an hour and a half as he was arriving to trade on

the north side of the island, getting close enough to hurl insults across the waves at the Englishmen, calling them 'dogs and rogues.' Harris eventually beached his sloop and managed to escape inland on foot, firing back at Rivero's men as they swarmed ashore to come to grips with him. His sloop was then refloated, and along with a canoe found on the beach, sailed away to Cuba.

A week later *Fama* and *Gallardina* returned, landing thirty men at Montego Bay to burn its coastal settlements, before retiring to Cuba

Above: Methods employed by buccaneers to discover their captives' hidden wealth – from declarations of Spanish slaves (right foreground), to other, more savage, means.

once more. On July 3rd Rivero was back a third time, having in the interim manned his captured English sloop with reinforcements from Santiago de Cuba. A company of forty mounted Jamaican militia watched this trio of Spanish corsair vessels for an hour, before they stood off to leeward. The next day the raiders landed fifty miles away and burnt a couple more houses, then the following night posted a written challenge on shore. In it, Rivero brazenly stated: 'I come to seek General Morgan with two ships of twenty guns, and having seen this, I crave he will come out upon the coast to seek me, that he might see the valour of the Spaniards.'

Rather than answer this challenge directly, Morgan and an incensed Jamaican Council opted for a full-blown retaliatory strike against some major target in Spanish America. Modyford felt constrained to agree, although his latest instructions still called for him to maintain peaceful relations with his Spanish neighbours. (His earlier complaints to London about the Spaniards' killing of Speirdyke, for example, had been unsympathetically dismissed with the observation that this was 'not at all to be wondered at, after such hostilities as your men have acted upon their territories.') Nevertheless the precedent of autonomous measures was still sufficiently well established at Port Royal to allow both the Governor and his Council to feel justified in passing a unanimous resolution on July 9th, commissioning Morgan 'to be Admiral and Commander-in-Chief of all the ships of war belonging to this harbour,' drawing them together into one fleet 'to attack, seize and destroy all the enemy's vessels that shall come within his reach.' Thus Rivero's nuisance raids were about to be repaid a hundredfold.

Morgan set sail from Port Royal on August 11th, at the head of a fleet of eleven vessels and six hundred men, his flag flying aboard *Satisfaction* of 120 tons (with its armament now augmented to 22 guns). He had further called for a great freebooter gathering at his favourite rendezvous off Île-à-Vache, to muster even more crushing strength. But first he ventured to the south coast of Cuba, where he left Morris's *Dolphin* on station to maintain a blockade, while standing away with his main body to recruit among the tough French *boucaniers* of Tortuga Island. As a result, Morgan did not actually gain his rendezvous off Île-à-Vache until September 12th, from where four days later he detached six more vessels under Edward Collier, to gather provisions and 'get prisoners for intelligence' on the Spanish Main.

The latter materialized off Río-hacha (in present-day Colombia) at daybreak on 24 October 1670, landing and marching his buccaneers against its tiny four-gun fortress with such a disciplined tread that the Spanish lookouts at first assumed these were regular troops out of England. This impression instantly faded once they beheld their dread West Indian foes drawing near, as the Spanish garrison included the crew of Rivero's consort vessel *Gallardina*, which was lying in the roads.

These Spanish corsairs were especially terrified at the prospect of falling into buccaneer hands, from whom they could expect little mercy, so they held out in desperation for a day and a night before surrendering. Their fears proved well founded, for Collier conducted a pair of cruel executions and tortured numerous captives so savagely that a Spanish eye-witness later exclaimed: 'In cold blood they did a thousand cursed things.' Satisfied with these brutal measures, Collier weighed almost four weeks later with a vast quantity of meat and maize, 38 prisoners, *Gallardina* and one other ship.

Meanwhile Morgan's fleet had been scattered by a storm off Île-à-Vache, but was slowly reassembling. During this interval his confederate Morris had rejoined from blockading Cuba, triumphantly bringing in Rivero's *Fama*, which he had seized after killing this hated Spanish cor-

Below: Troops marching across open country.

sair. The encounter had occurred in mid-October, when Morris had been forced to put into a small bay at the east end of Cuba with his 10-gun *Dolphin* and sixty-man crew, because of a threatening storm. Two hours later, just before dark, Rivero had sailed in for this same purpose with his 14-gun *Fama*, and been delighted to find the smaller Jamaican ship entrapped. Setting men ashore to cut off any possibilities of escape overland, the corsair had then confidently prepared to attack at dawn.

But it was Morris who struck first the next morning, bearing down upon *Fama* with the land breeze, and boarding at the first attempt. Rivero was shot through the neck and died in a pool of blood, panicking his crew who then jumped into the sea, where some drowned and many others were slaughtered by the English privateers. Only five Spaniards were left to be plucked alive from these crimson-stained waters, after which *Fama* had been mockingly renamed the *Lamb*, and paraded jubilantly before the buccaneer throng at Île-à-Vache.

But although Jamaica's principal tormentor had been slain and his two vessels seized, there was no let-up to Morgan's massive preparations. The opportunity of plundering a major Spanish-American port was too tempting to resist, so that captains from many different nationalities continued to arrive, drawn by this sanctioned operation during a period of relative slackness throughout the West Indies. One such rover was Robert Searle, ironically released from detention at Port Royal, where he had been briefly arrested by Modyford for attacking Spanish Saint Augustine. Another was Dutch-born Laurens Prins, who in a singularly bold venture had slipped up Colombia's Magdalena River with Captains Harris and Ludbury, intending to surprise the important town of Mompós, although it was 150 miles removed from the sea. This daring attempt had been foiled when a fort was discovered recently constructed on an island in that river.

Undeterred, this trio had then veered westward to the Mosquito Coast, hoping to find better hunting there. Ascending the San Juan River (despite the fort which had also been installed on that waterway since Morgan's raid five years earlier), Prins and his cohorts stole across the Lake of Nicaragua and took the city of Granada. According to a Spanish account, Prins 'made havoc and a thousand destructions,' driving home his demands for ransom by 'sending the head of a priest in a basket and saying that he would deal with the rest of the prisoners in the same way, unless they gave him 70,000 pesos.'

A few weeks later he was back at Port Royal, where Modyford reproved him mildly for attacking the Spaniards without commission, but thought it prudent not 'to press the matter too far in this juncture.' Instead he ordered Prins and his followers to go join Morgan, 'which they were very ready to do.' Prins incorporated his ship *Pearl* of ten guns and fifty men into the latter's fleet, and because of his fierce reputation and previous friendship with the admiral, was considered a senior officer.

By the time Morgan's expedition finally weighed on December 18th, he had 38 vessels and more than two thousand English, French and Dutch freebooters under his command, the largest buccaneer enterprise mounted until that time. He had chosen Panama as his primary objective (perhaps because of his previous dealings with its President), but first touched at tiny Providencia Island en route, which the Spaniards had reconquered from Edward Mansfield's isolated garrison some years previously. Consequently, early on December 24th, Morgan's huge fleet appeared before this place, forcing its Spanish defenders to surrender the next day by sheer weight of numbers.

Three days later Morgan detached a trio of ships and 470 men to sail ahead of his fleet and seize the vital San Lorenzo fort guarding the mouth of the Chagres River, where he intended to land and use it as an advance base for his march across the Isthmus toward Panama. Command of this force was assigned to the veteran privateersman Joseph Bradley, with a commission as 'Lieutenant-Colonel;' his 70-ton *Mayflower* was to serve as squadron flagship, accompanied by 'Major' Richard Norman's 10-gun *Lilly*, and Dutch-born Jelles de Lecat's *Seviliaen*. These three hove into view of that fortification at noon on 6 January 1671, disembarking four hundred freebooters who advanced briskly 'with flags and trumpets' displayed under the bright tropical sun, making their attack that afternoon.

Believing they had caught the Spaniards unprepared, the raiders seriously underestimated the opposition. Awaiting them was a recently-reinforced garrison of 360 soldiers, whose *castellano* or fortress commander Pedro de Elizalde had been so inspired by his greater strength as to exult to his superiors: 'Even if all England were to come, they would not capture this castle.' Much to Bradley's astonishment, his first and second charges were halted by a deadly hail of bullets, so that as dusk fell he was constrained to lead his men creeping forward through some gullies, close enough to toss grenades and fire-pots inside the fort. These succeeded in igniting its wooden stockades, gradually spreading throughout that night until they had consumed much of the defenses, and detonated most of San Lorenzo's magazines.

In the resultant smoke and darkness some 150 Spanish soldiers chose to desert, but enough remained at their posts the next day to break Bradley's assaults. Finally a contingent of French *flibustiers* from Tortuga managed to fight their way inside on the fifth attempt, and a badly wounded Bradley could hear them shouting '*Victoire! Victoire!*' above the murderous din. Elizalde and his remaining seventy defenders fought bravely to the last man, before being massacred. No pity was shown, as at least thirty buccaneers had been killed and another 76 injured during these assaults, including Bradley, who was shot through both legs. Norman assumed overall command of the devastated fort while his superior convalesced, but five days later – just as Morgan's masts were rising above the horizon – the 'Lieutenant-Colonel' died of his wounds.

Satisfaction led Morgan's fleet into this hard-won anchorage on January 12th, only to strike a hidden reef at its entrance and plunge to the bottom, taking the next four vessels in line down with it as well. Ten men drowned, but otherwise losses were rather minimal, and soon after his entire army was ashore. A week was spent refurbishing the burnt fortress and installing a strong new garrison of three hundred buccaneers under Norman, before Morgan at last felt ready to take the final, irrevocable step of probing upriver with at least 1,500 men in seven small ships, and 36 boats.

The power and audacity of the West Indian buccaneers had now reached a new plateau, being so swollen that they were willing to penetrate deep into Spanish territory – even as far as the remote Pacific shore, well removed from their anchored ships and which most had never seen before – in the fullest expectation of achieving victory. Much of this confidence had to do with their leader, whom they believed to have shrewdly gauged the enemy's weaknesses; but it was also founded upon their own frequent successes against larger Spanish American formations, whose

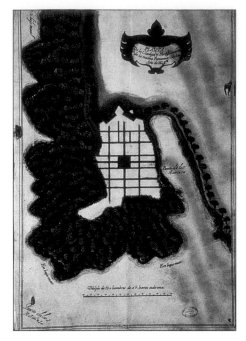

Above: Spanish view of Panama as it appeared in 1675, four years after being ruthlessly sacked by Morgan. Note that north lies to the right of this map. (Archivo General de Indias, Seville, Spain)

superior numbers could be defeated by a combination of surprise, mobility, and disciplined firepower. Indeed, during this forthcoming campaign only the torrid climate, dense vegetation and lack of suffi-

cient water or provisions would prove serious obstacles to the invaders, as the Panamanians themselves proved incapable of launching any effective counter-attacks, despite the threat to their homes and loved ones.

A gruelling seven-day trek ensued for Morgan's buccaneers, thrashing through marshy channels and faintly marked jungle trails, until finally at nine o'clock on the morning of Tuesday, 27 January 1671, his vanguard crested a hill and saw 'that desired place, the South Sea' shimmering in the distance, with a galleon and several smaller vessels riding upon it. Towards noon the invaders came upon a great plain filled with cattle, which they slaughtered and paused to eat. Thus refreshed, they pressed on and that afternoon sighted the red tiled roofs of Panama City itself, with a Spanish army drawn up at Mata Asnillos, a mile outside its gates, to bar their path.

The 52-year-old local Governor Juan Pérez de Guzmán, Knight of the Order of Santiago, had succeeded in mustering this force

Below: View of the main square at Panama. (Archivo General de Indias, Seville, Spain)

despite being painfully afflicted with 'Saint Anthony's fire' (erysipelas, a contagious skin disease caused by streptococcus, whose symptoms included both boils and high fever). Despite the large tumour spreading on his right breast and repeated bleedings by his physician, Pérez de Guzmán had several days earlier attempted to waylay Morgan's progress at Guayabal, riding forth with eight hundred militiamen from Panama, only to have two-thirds of these desert during the night. Retiring once more into his city, the Spanish Governor then resorted to ordering all able-bodied citizens to gather just outside its gates, while noncombatants were to be evacuated by ship.

On the evening of the 27th, Morgan's vanguard moved into view, and the waiting Spaniards could clearly see the after-effects of the wine that this fearsome horde had looted at the nearby town of Venta de Cruces. 'We have nothing to fear,' a Spanish officer laughed con-temptuously to the militiamen around him. 'There are no more than six hundred drunkards!' But more buccaneer companies continued to arrive after nightfall, so that – inebriated or not – by next morning double that number had assembled.

Morgan began his final advance at sunrise on the 28th, with 'red and green banners and flags clearly visible to the Spaniards who awaited them on the plain a couple of miles away'. Pérez de Guzmán had 1,200 militia infantry drawn up in a long line, six deep, with two militia cavalry companies of two hundred riders apiece on both flanks. But the Governor knew his inexperienced troops had few firearms and no artillery between them, so would prove no match for the veteran, better-armed invaders. Rather forlornly, he pinned his hopes of breaking Morgan's formation on the ancient tactic of stampeding great herds of cattle through their ranks.

However, the buccaneer vanguard – under Prins's direction – swung round the Spaniards' right flank to gain the high ground, whereupon Pérez de Guzmán's unwieldy host suddenly launched a wild, premature dash against the enemy lines. Prins's men received this Spanish charge with concentrated fusillades, more than one hundred militiamen being mown down by the first volley. 'Hardly did our men see some fall dead and others wounded,' Pérez de Guzmán later declared, 'but they turned their backs and fled.'

He himself rode into their midst with his staff raised high 'like a mast', hoping to rally his troops, but this was impossible. Given such a one-sided exchange of gunfire, in which 400–500 Spaniards were quickly killed or wounded as opposed to only fifteen buccaneers, the defenders' courage naturally melted away, and soon a pell-mell flight began. Pérez de Guzmán rode disconsolately through the city streets, shouting to the few remaining inhabitants that all was lost, before joining the last refugees streaming out the far gate, while buildings were set ablaze as Morgan's victorious army entered to take possession.

Panama was now entirely in buccaneer hands, but proved a hollow prize. Its buildings lay empty and abandoned, most of its riches having long since been removed to the ships offshore, who now stood away from the coast, once the outcome to this battle had become obvious.

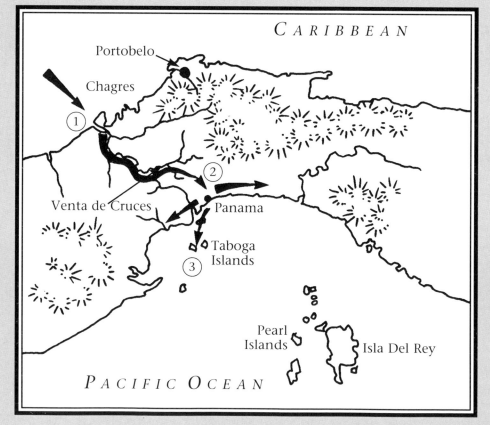

Left: Morgan's Panama Campaign (December 1670 to January 1671): After seizing Chagres (1), Morgan's army marched on Panama via Venta de Cruces, defeating the forces gathered before its gates (2). He then detached columns of looters to scour the surrounding countryside, one of which narrowly missed capturing the immensely wealthy galleon *Santísima Trinidad* off Taboga Island (3).

DELINEACION DE LA TIERRA, Y CIUDAD DE PANAMA.

CIUDAD DE PANAMA

Above: Map of Morgan's line of march across the Isthmus of Panama: north is towards the bottom, with the town of Chagres misspelled 'Cagre'. From here, the invading host followed the winding Chagres River all the way to Venta de Cruces (centre), before making its final advance against Panama City (upper left, beneath compass rose).

Thus the freebooters' greatest military foray was to prove their bitterest disappointment: for although they had harnessed sufficient strength and numbers to conquer a major Spanish American city, its meagre plunder could not hope to satisfy their expanded membership. Aware of this problem, Morgan promptly delegated patrols to scour the surrounding countryside, but here his legendary luck at last forsook him.

One such unit was commanded by Robert Searle, who at Morgan's behest took a tiny flotilla of commandeered coastal craft to ransack the offshore islands. At Taboga, Searle and his men came upon a large cache of wine, which by that evening they were well on their way to consuming. In their drunkenness they failed to post lookouts, and so did not notice when the 400-ton *Santísima Trinidad* ('Most Blessed Trinity') of Captain Francisco de Peralta circled back to that island from farther out in the Gulf. This galleon had departed Panama earlier with *San Felipe Neri*, between them carrying the bulk of the Spaniards' valuables and non-combatants. Unaware that the triumphant raiders had now spread this far out from the mainland, De Peralta sent a seven-man party ashore to ease the suffering of his passengers by securing water.

These unfortunate few blundered into a group of buccaneers, who captured them and brought them before Searle. Threatened with torture, they revealed the presence of this extremely wealthy prize nearby, but by the time the befuddled privateer chieftain and his men could react, De Peralta had become suspicious at the failure of his watering party to return and steered his galleon back into the night. When Morgan's main army learned of this missed opportunity a few days later, their wrath could scarcely be contained. Even writing several years after this event, the chronicler Exquemelin could not refrain from scornfully describing how when these captives had been brought before Searle, the old pirate 'had been more inclined to sit drinking and sporting with a group of Spanish women he had taken prisoner, than to go at once in pursuit of the treasure ship'.

As their hopes of instant wealth gradually dimmed, Morgan's men resorted to ever crueller methods

Buccaneer Weapons

The rovers' rise to world-wide predominance during the second half of the seventeenth century can be attributed primarily to one factor: firepower. No matter how few in numbers, most pirate bands felt they could carry any objective through guile, mobility and superior musketry. This was not only true on land, but in ship-to-ship encounters as well, where a dozen well-aimed muskets were held to be the equivalent of a heavy gun. (Rather than attacking with a broadside of roundshot, French *flibustiers'* favoured a volley of musketry followed by a boarding-party, their prizes being less likely to sustain grievous damage.)

Given the absence of armament factories and powder-mills in the Americas during this period, most weaponry had to be imported from Holland, France or England. This gave the West Indian privateers a distinct advantage over their Spanish–American foes, for whom firearms remained an expensive luxury because of Madrid's more antiquated trade policies – thus hampering their colonies' defensive capabilities, while at the same time contributing to the buc-caneers' increasing arrogance, as the latter came to believe all Spaniards were easy prey.

The buccaneers equipped themselves with the best firearms they could obtain, and in considerable profusion. For example, the members of the expedition which Laurens de Graaf and the Sieur de Grammont led against Veracruz in May 1683 were instructed to bring as many firearms with them as possible, in order to offset the defenders' heavier numbers. During the attack itself, more than one inhabitant noticed how the raiders brushed aside its garrison because each 'carried three or four firearms', while later, when thousands of Spanish captives were being herded on to Sacrificios Island, they were guarded by a few score pirates, 'each one with three firearms and a short sword or cutlass'.

With the exception of Saint-Domingue's *boucaniers* and other such sharpshooting hunters, most privateersmen waited until they could unleash volleys from close range during battle. For this reason they were often armed with either a musket or blunderbuss, plus two or more pistols for

Below: Typical pistol of the period. **Right:** Musket drill.

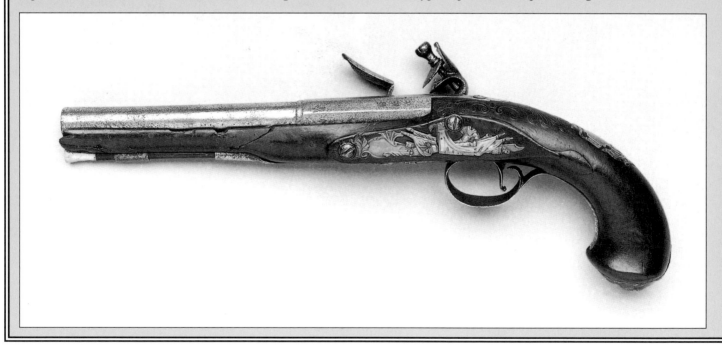

with the captives who fell into their hands, angrily probing for hidden treasure; but despite the extreme savagery meted out, little more plunder could be produced. After four weeks' fruitless occupation, the army abandoned this unhappy city and retraced its steps back across the Isthmus. When the final division of spoils was made at Chagres, the surly rank-and-file discovered that they were to receive only £15 or £18 a head, so that to general disillusionment was added a nagging suspicion that they had been cheated by their leaders. In light of this ugly mood, Morgan departed Chagres hastily on 16 March 1671 aboard the dead Bradley's *Mayflower*, accompanied by only three vessels commanded by his most loyal captains. It was to be his last campaign.

Upon reaching Port Royal a couple of weeks later, he found England's policy unmistakably altered. A new treaty had been signed with Madrid, so that attacks against Spanish America were now most definitely out of favour. Three months later, HMSS *Assistance* and *Welcome* arrived with a new Governor for that island – 39-year-old Sir Thomas Lynch, a pronounced Hispanophile who had spent an entire winter living in Salamanca to perfect his command of this

Blow your match.

Try your match.

Give Fire.

point-blank work (the effects of this latter fire being so murderous that the term 'pistol-proof' became a byword among buccaneers, to denote anything invincible or outstanding). For the rest, rovers would carry additional charges – nicknamed 'apostles', perhaps because these usually numbered a dozen – in their bandoliers or cartridge belts, plus the usual vicious assortment of swords, dirks and axes for hand-to-hand combat.

In lieu of artillery, their land forays often involved the use of grenades, a particularly favoured assault weapon. Not wishing to be encumbered, the pirates substituted hand-grenades for siege-guns in order to sow confusion and panic within enemy fortifications, or redoubts. For example, during this same attack on Veracruz, a contingent of forty buccaneers rushed the northern Caleta bastion at dawn, tossing grenades through its apertures before swarming on to the rooftop. The resultant detonations were so loud that they could be heard three-quarters of a mile away on San Juan de Ulúa island, and caused the bastion to surrender immediately, without a struggle.

Grenades could be made of either iron or glass. The French chronicler and priest Jean-Baptiste Labat recorded an instance of this latter usage, when the *flibustiers* of Capitaine Pinel swarmed over the bows of a British 18-gun ship off Barbados in early 1694 (during the War of the League of Augsburg, known in America as King William's War). The English crew barricaded itself inside the forecastle, but Pinel's boarders found a small hatch:

... through which they flung a glass jar filled with gunpowder and surrounded by four or five lit fuses, which ignited the powder when the jar burst and burned seven or eight Englishmen so horribly, they called for quarter.

language – and who informed Modyford that he was to be arrested to assuage Spanish complaints. A like gesture was required when news of Morgan's devastating raid against Panama reached Europe a little while later, so that in November 1671 Lynch was ordered to arrest the former 'admiral' as well.

But by then the new Governor was reluctant to proceed, for hostilities were once more on the rise in the West Indies, and he was loath to alienate the privateers on whom Jamaica depended for its defence. Like so many high-minded reformers before him, Lynch was forced to acknowledge the vital role these played in preserving the island for the Crown. He therefore decided to send Morgan home in such a manner 'as he shall not be much disgusted', and further deferred the actual arrest for several months because of the rover's alleged poor health.

It was not until mid-April 1672 that the great freebooter was at last conducted aboard the 36-gun royal frigate *Welcome* of Captain John Keene, to sail for England as escort for a three-ship convoy.

Three months later they arrived at Spithead, and because Morgan continued 'very sickly,' he was not imprisoned upon reaching London that August, but rather housed at his own expense. However, his sliding fortunes finally began to right themselves, when this also proved to be the same summer that the Third Anglo-Dutch War erupted in Europe, with England and France ranged together in an alliance against The Netherlands. Given such distractions, there was little urgency to prosecute Morgan, especially when Spain was later drawn into this conflict on the opposing side. All of which gradually produced a complete reversal in Whitehall's policies, while at the same time Morgan was able to use his extended period of liberty to meet with the young Duke of Albemarle, who interceded on his behalf with Charles II.

By the end of July 1673, Morgan's position had so improved that he was being asked to submit a memorandum to the King, describing what measures would be required to better ensure Jamaica's safety. In January 1674 the Council of Trade and Plantations further decided to recall the pro-Spanish Lynch and replace him with the 43-year-old dilettante John, Lord Vaughan, Morgan being seconded to this rather dissolute young peer as an experienced Deputy Governor. Such a position naturally called for a title, so in November 1674 Morgan was knighted, and next spring sailed for Jamaica. By now England had withdrawn from the on-going wars between France, Spain and Holland, so that a new generation of leaders was emerging in that lush but merciless cockpit known as the West Indies.

Opposite page, top: Seventeenth-century soldier firing a musket.

Opposite page, bottom: Hand grenades were a favourite weapon of West Indian buccaneers. Here we see a French soldier demonstrating how to ignite one, from a 1686 military manual.

Above: Morgan recruiting followers, as envisaged by the American illustrator Howard Pyle.

Right: Portrait of the mature, sly-eyed villain – Sir Henry Morgan, presumably as he appeared during his exile in England, 1672–4

V

Rise of the Flibustiers

They beat the men, and burnt the town,
Then all the baggage was their own.
John Wilmot, Earl of Rochester (1647–1680)

ngland's retirement from the Third Anglo-Dutch War in the spring of 1674 had unwittingly paved the way for another European nation to secure the allegiance of its West Indian privateers. Because France had been left so weak at sea, once the Royal Navy withdrew from these hostilities the French officials were willing to dispense privateering licences with a liberal hand; their colonial representatives in the remote Caribbean proved especially eager, as their own regional forces had suffered a serious setback at the very outset of this conflict.

When Governor-General Jean-Charles de Baas-Castelmore of the Windward Islands had learned of his country's declaration of war against Holland, he quickly began to organise an expedition to attack the Dutch stronghold of Curaçao. For this purpose he detached the 50-gun *Ecueil* ('Reef') and the smaller *Petite Infante* ('Little Infanta' or 'Spanish Princess') to Saint-Domingue, with orders for that island's Governor Bertrand d'Ogeron to raise a large number of volunteers from among its *boucaniers*, and join the Governor-General's main body off Saint Croix on 4 March 1673.

But as these particular two warships and half-a-dozen lesser buccaneer craft began forging their way back around Puerto Rico toward this rendezvous on the night of 25/26 February 1673, a navigational error caused *Ecueil* to run aground in the vicinity of Arecibo, where more than half her people were lost. Five hundred survivors managed to struggle ashore through the surf, only to be interned by the local Spaniards. Such a devastating loss gave even greater impetus to the commissions which were already being issued to some British rovers, who besides being recent partners in the war against Holland, were always eager to fight the Spaniards.

John Bennett was one such freebooter, using his twenty-man Jamaican brigantine to intercept the 50-ton frigate *Buen Jesús de las Almas* (literally, 'Good Jesus of the Souls'), as it was approaching the coast of Santo Domingo in April 1675, with 46,471 pieces of eight as payroll or *situado* for that island's garrison. The Spanish authorities protested to Whitehall, who rejected this complaint by pointing out that Bennett 'had Frenchmen on board, a French commission, fought under French colours, [and] had the prize condemned and adjudged in French ports'.

Nevertheless the British Crown felt constrained to restrict their nationals from brazenly serving as foreign mercenaries throughout the remainder of this conflict, as they realised such activities might cast Britain's neutrality in a suspicious light. Haughty Lord Vaughan, the newly installed Governor at Jamaica, was one official who would find particular difficulty in getting the members of this independent-minded brotherhood to comply.

On 13 April 1675, shortly after his inauguration, he issued a proclamation offering amnesty to all that island's privateers, if they would return and renounce roving. Naturally this had little effect, with commissions from the three other belligerents being temptingly available throughout the Caribbean. Vaughan was further disillusioned by Morgan's apparent lack of influence, whom he had assumed would command the freebooters' blind obedience. When this did not materialise, he became convinced that his deputy was conniving with the renegades behind his back, and wrote to London that: 'Sir Henry, contrary to his duty and trust, endeavours to set up privateering, and has obstructed all my designs and purposes as to those who do use that curse of life.'

This false accusation caused a rift with Morgan, yet otherwise did nothing to alleviate the Governor's problem. Jamaican rovers continued to operate under foreign flags, so that when in the spring of 1676 a mercenary named John Deane was accused of intercepting the merchant ship *John Adventure* on the high seas, and 'drunk out several pipes of wine and taken away a cable value £100', Vaughan instructed Morgan 'to imprison the offenders'

Above: French *boucaniers* or *Frères de la Coste* ('Brethren of the Coast'), c. 1665, by Tillac.

on a charge of piracy. The latter obeyed, but only grudgingly, for like many other people at Port Royal he felt that Deane's mischief did not warrant such a serious charge.

None the less this captive was brought before Vaughan in his capacity of judge in late April 1676, when it was revealed that he had also sailed 'wearing Dutch, French, and Spanish colours without lawful commission,' for which he was condemned to death. This verdict did not sit well with the public, and the Governor soon heard how 'since the trial Sir Harry has been so impudent and unfaithful at the taverns and in his own house, to speak some things which seemed to reflect upon my justice, and to vindicate the pirate'. But Morgan was not alone in this opinion, and Vaughan's resolve soon wavered. He was forced to pardon Deane several months later on direct instructions from London, and then had to watch in growing frustration as the British freeboot-

Above: French *flibustiers* aboard a tiny yacht.

ers continued their foreign depredations.

In June 1677 a mixed band of buccaneers, under the command of a French captain named La Garde, captured Santa Marta on the Spanish Main. This *flibustier* force surprised that town at dawn and took many captives, including its governor and bishop, holding these for ransom until a trio of Armada de Barlovento warships appeared from Cartagena with five hundred soldiers to drive them off. The raiders then retired towards Port Royal, and on 28 July 1677 Sir Thomas Lynch noted in his diary:

Five or six French and English privateers lately come to Jamaica from taking Santa Marta, [William] Barnes being one and [John] Coxon expected every hour. On board the Governor and the Bishop,

and Captain Legarde [*sic*] has promised to put them on shore. The plunder of the town was not great, money and broken plate [*i.e.*, silver] about £20 a man.

Three days later Coxon entered port, and personally escorted the Spanish bishop and a friar into Vaughan's presence. On the Governor's orders, this prelate was nobly housed, and British officers were sent aboard the buccaneer flotilla to attempt 'to procure the liberty of the [Spanish] Governor and others, but finding the privateers all drunk, it was impossible to persuade them to do anything by fair means'. Vaughan therefore ordered the French to quit Port Royal entirely, and officially advised Coxon and his British followers that it was now against the law for them to serve under foreign colours. He observed

that the French were 'damnably enraged' at being deprived of their English companions, so much so that they sailed off without releasing their other captives.

That winter, however, French naval power achieved a resounding victory over the Dutch at Tobago, when Vice-Admiral Jean, comte d'Estrées, destroyed the remnant of Admiral Jacob Binckes's smaller fleet on 12 December 1677. Flush with this triumph, the French commander-in-chief spent the next five months gathering a massive expedition to wipe out the last remaining Dutch outpost in the West Indies, Curaçao. For this venture his eighteen royal warships were reinforced by two thousand buccaneer auxiliaries, all of whom stood

Right: Portrait of the French Vice-Admiral Jean, comte d'Estrées, whose haughty disregard for his pilots' advice led to a massive shipwreck on Aves Islands, thereby freeing his *flibustier* auxiliaries for an independent thrust into the Laguna de Maracaibo.

out of Martinique together on 7 May 1678.

But the arrogant d'Estrées had chosen a course closely parallel to the South American coast, despite warnings from the local pilots that these were dangerously shoal waters. At 9 o'clock on the evening of the 11th, one of his *flibustier* consorts suddenly began firing muskets, followed immediately by a gun, in a frantic attempt to signal that his fleet was sailing on to the reefs surrounding the Aves Islands group. This warning came too late; seven ships of the line, three transports, and three corsair vessels had their bottoms ripped out and sank, including d'Estrées's own flagship *Terrible*, with a total loss of five hundred lives. His forces thrown away in this needless disaster, the water-logged admiral was left with no choice but to retire towards Saint-Domingue with his survivors, greatly embittered to see the heartless *flibustiers* scavenging among the wreckage of his dead fleet.

Now left to their own devices, the latter adopted an alternate plan of leapfrogging past Curaçao, to materialise in the Gulf of Venezuela during the first days of June 1678. Their six large ships and thirteen lighter ones were led by a small, dark, active individual destined to become one of the greatest commanders of the Brethren of the Coast – the 'Chevalier' de Grammont. His bravery, quick wit and open-handedness had already made him a favourite among the tough *boucaniers* of Saint-Domingue, a contemporary noting: 'He has a particular secret for winning their hearts, and insinuating himself into

their spirits.' It was Grammont's intent to duplicate the earlier feats of Nau l'Olonnais and Morgan, by leading a destructive rampage through the Laguna de Maracaibo.

Confronted by the rebuilt fortress guarding its Bar, he disembarked half his men and marched along the San Carlos peninsula toward its landward face. The Spanish garrison commander, Francisco Pérez de Guzmán, was only able to prevent an immediate assault by stationing some one hundred arquebusiers outside its walls, but heavy siege guns were then manhandled ashore from the buccaneer flotilla, so that after a brief bombardment the

Spanish defenders were forced to surrender. The victorious Grammont promptly passed his ships over the Bar, leaving the six largest to blockade the entrance while he pressed on towards Maracaibo with the other thirteen.

This oft-victimised city and its outlying area were thrown into utter panic by the news of this latest incursion, so that the new Governor – the ancient and sickly Jorge Madureira Ferreira, who had only been installed in office a week before – was unable to inspire any confidence in his outnumbered troops. People began fleeing in every direction, soon followed by Madureira himself, who retired to the inland town of Maicao with his handful of regulars. Thus Grammont occupied Maracaibo unopposed on 14 June, and gave it over to the sack. A Spanish eye-witness said of him: 'This French enemy

Above: Large-scale seventeenth-century disembarkation, by the Spanish court painter Zurbarán. (El Prado Museum, Madrid)

Left: Grammont's Maracaibo Campaign (June to December 1678): In summer 1678, Grammont appeared in the Gulf of Venezuela with two thousand buccaneers aboard six large ships, and thirteen smaller ones. After forcing the surrender of the fort defending the San Carlos bar (1), he left his capital ships behind to guard this entrance, while pressing on toward Maracaibo (2) with the remainder. Having ransacked this city and its surrounding area, he took Gibraltar (3), then pressed deeper inland to the city of Trujillo (4), which he stormed on 1 September. Retiring to Gibraltar, he torched this place on the 25th, before ensconcing himself in Maracaibo until early December, when he departed for Saint Domingue (5) with enormous booty.

Right: The 'Chevalier' de Grammont, as depicted by Tillac.

was so tyrannical that after taking everything people had, he would torture them unto death, something which not even a Turk or a Moor would do.'

Skilled in military deployment, Grammont took horses from the deserted stables and organised mounted *flibustier* columns which struck out in pursuit of the Spanish leaders and scattered them even farther afield. On 28 June he quit the gutted remains of Maracaibo to cross to the south-eastern shores of the Laguna, and fall upon Gibraltar. This town too was already quite deserted, and after a token bombardment of its walls the gar-

rison of only 22 soldiers gave up.

Emboldened by this total lack of opposition, Grammont pressed deeper inland, marching almost fifty miles to the town of Trujillo, which was defended by a regular fort manned by 350 troops and four artillery pieces. Again he prevailed – much to the Spaniards' horror – by

storming this fortification on 1 September from the rear, 'by some hills where it seemed impossible to do so', according to one disheartened defender. Again terrified Spanish citizens crowded the roads, straggling 75 miles south-westward into the town of Mérida de la Grita, hoping to escape from this implacable raider.

Having thus defeated or dispersed every large Spanish concentration he had met, Grammont retraced his steps toward the Laguna, re-entering Gibraltar after a leisurely sack of the countryside. This unfortunate town was then stripped bare and put to the torch on 25 September, although the invading host otherwise evinced no great haste to depart the region. Openly contemptuous of the Spaniards' ability to retaliate, they remained ensconced along the shores of the Laguna de Maracaibo till almost the end of that year.

It was not until 3 December 1678 that Grammont finally sailed away, presumably because there was nothing left to eat, drink or break in those luckless provinces. His ships returned to Petit-Goâve on Christmas Eve, engorged with booty and captives, and he and his men embarked upon a riotous festival of drink and debauchery. Well might the *flibustiers* celebrate, for although their countrymen were at last winding down their war in Europe, local frictions would continue to give the American privateers ample employment for many years to come.

John Coxon, for one, soon resumed his activities, by leading a mixed party of British, French and other marauders out of Jamaica on a foray into the Bay of Honduras where, on 26 September 1679, they

Above: Grammont's unexpected use of cavalry after the seizure of Maracaibo.

captured a Spanish merchantman laden with 'five hundred chests of indigo, a great quantity of cacao, cochineal, tortoise shell, money and plate'. After disposing of this booty somewhat clandestinely in Jamaica, Coxon held an illegal assemblage at Port Morant, during which he recruited four other captains for an assault against the Panamanian port of Portobelo.

These five vessels quit Port Morant on 17 January 1680, and less than twenty miles out at sea met the brigantine of the French *flibustier* Jean Rose, who also joined the expedition and furnished it with the necessary commissions from the Governor of Saint-Domingue. The ships then made their way to the San Bernardo or 'Friends' Islands near Cartagena on the Spanish Main, where they stole 'four *piraguas* and six very good large canoes' to use as landing-craft. This done, the formation proceeded towards Isla de Pinos (literally 'Island of Pines,' 130 miles east of Portobelo in the Archipelago de las Mulatas, off Panama's north-eastern coast), where Coxon transferred 250 buccaneers into his boats and began rowing westward along that coast, hoping to strike before the Spaniards could learn of his presence.

Nearing his goal he came upon 'a great ship riding at anchor' which proved to be that of another *flibustier* commander, Capitaine Lessone, who added eighty Frenchmen to the boat parties. Shortly afterwards the buccaneers slipped ashore in the Gulf of San Blas, proceeding afoot to avoid the local Spanish coastal watchers. They marched three days 'without any food, and their feet cut with the rocks for want of shoes', until on 7 February they came upon an Indian village three miles short of Portobelo. Here a native spotted them and shouted '*Ladrones!*' ('Thieves!'), before setting off at a run towards the distant city.

Coxon's buccaneers trotted painfully in pursuit, but the Indian arrived fully half an hour before them and raised the alarm. Nevertheless the attackers' vanguard was able to sweep in unopposed, as the Spaniards were caught so unprepared that they withdrew into their citadel and left the raiders to ransack Portobelo unhindered over the next two days. Coxon then retired his small army ten miles north-eastward, entrenching with his booty and a few prisoners on a cay half a mile offshore from the town of Bastimentos, while a boat was sent to recall the anchored ships. Three days later several hundred Spanish troops appeared and began firing upon the pirates from the beach,

but were unable to exact any vengeance before the vessels arrived to rescue the intruders.

Coxon then returned to institute a sea blockade of Portobelo, intercepting a couple of unsuspecting ships which arrived, before finally making a general distribution of booty that resulted in shares of one hundred pieces of eight per man. Afterwards he and his confederates retired to Bocas del Toro to careen their ships because 'of its good store of turtle and manatee and fish', according to one contented rover. A couple more Jamaican privateering sloops joined Coxon before he gave the order for all eight vessels to

Above: Scenes from the life of a *boucanier*, with his hunting dogs. Although crack shots and quite fearless, these men lacked proper military discipline.

return to Golden Island and avail themselves of their friendship with the local Indians 'to travel overland to Panama' and attack the Spaniards on their Pacific flank. The British all agreed, but the French under Lessone and Rose refused, preferring to prowl the Gulf of San Blas again. Thus the two contingents parted amicably in early April 1680.

Little more than three months later, at the end of that July, a Spanish emissary visited Jacques Nepveu, sieur de Pouançay and Governor of the French half of Saint-Domingue, with a copy of the Treaty of Nijmegen recently ratified between France and Spain, as well as a private letter from the Governor of Santo Domingo calling for peace. The only condition the Spaniard added was that Pouançay 'restrain and contain the subjects of France that inhabit Tortuga', specifically prohibiting them from landing on the shores of Santo Domingo.

Pouançay rejected this proposal by pointing out that the peace treaty (like previous agreements negotiated by Spain with England) contained 'no article concerning the affairs of this government [*i.e.*, Saint-Domingue]', and so had been deliberately crafted by Madrid to avoid any legal standing for the French settlements in the New World. Pouançay concluded his reply by saying that he was willing to live in peace with his Spanish neighbours, but would not place unreasonable restraints upon the movements of French citizens, who had been inhabiting long stretches of Santo Domingo's north and western shores for more than forty years.

Privately, Pouançay informed his superiors in Paris that he doubted the sincerity of this offer, as French merchantmen continued to be snapped up by Spanish *guardacostas* and carried into port. Consequently he intended to maintain his hard line against what he perceived to be untrustworthy enemies, further motivated by his belief that the riches brought in by the 1,000–1,200 *flibustiers* operating out of Saint-Domingue were vital for that colony's economic survival.

As its population only totalled 7,800 people at this time – including many indentured servants or *engagés*, as well as slaves, yet relatively few prosperous planters or traders – this notion was not entirely far-fetched. In the words of the Governor: 'What the *flibustiers* take is employed here, and their silver passes to France.' Moreover, he did not wish to see these profits going elsewhere, to strengthen some rival outpost at Saint-Domingue's expense, such as Jamaica, Curaçao, the Virginias, New England or Florida. He therefore would continue his policy of liberally granting commissions to privateers of all nations, even after word of this treaty had reached him, because of his desire to entice both their trade and fierce martial qualities into his colony.

This decision would eventually lead to France's recruitment of one of the most gifted sea-rovers of this, or any other age – Laurens Cornelis Boudewijn de Graaf. Originally born in Holland, this adventurer had served three years as a lowly gunner in Spain's Armada de Barlovento, before deserting in the Antilles. According to Pouançay, De Graaf began roving on the account and by 1676 or 1677 had established himself as a leader among the wild, untamed *boucaniers* of Samaná Bay, 'never having wanted to take out a commission from anyone', nor 'put into the port of any nation'.

The French Governor went on to describe De Graaf's rise as a pirate: 'From a small bark, he took a small ship; from this a bigger one, until at last there came into his power one of 24 to 28 guns.' This latter was the ship *Tigre*, which De Graaf had wrested from his former Armada de Barlovento employers in the autumn of 1679 off the Spanish Main. By the spring of 1682 his exploits had achieved such notoriety that even Morgan, in his capacity as Acting Governor of Jamaica, had been moved to call him 'a great and mischievous pirate'.

This new buccaneer chieftain was described by a contemporary observer as tall, blonde and handsome, with a spiked Spanish-style moustache 'which suited him very well'. It was further added:

He always carries violins and trumpets aboard with which to entertain himself and amuse others who derive pleasure from this. He is further distinguished amongst filibusters by his courtesy and good taste. Overall he has won such fame that when it is known he has arrived at some place, many come from all around to see with their own eyes whether 'Lorenzo' is made like other men.

In July 1682, De Graaf's *Tigre* materialised off Puerto Rico's western shore, intent on ambushing yet another Armada de Barlovento frigate, the 30-gun *Princesa* (formerly the French *Dauphine*, more commonly called '*Francesa*' by the Spaniards).

This man-of-war stood unsuspectingly out of the Mona Passage, outward bound from Havana under Captain Manuel Delgado to deliver 120,000 pesos as the annual payrolls for the garrisons of Puerto Rico and Santo Domingo, as well as sundry lesser stores. Its decks a-clutter in anticipation of making landfall at Aguada, Puerto Rico, *Francesa* was taken utterly aback by De Graaf's appearance, fifty of her 250-man crew being killed or wounded in the resultant battle. The triumphant Dutchman and his *boucanier* crew repaired with this prize to their lair at Samaná Bay, where they allegedly 'made 140 shares and shared 700 pieces of eight a man', a very rich haul at the cost of only a few casualties. The Spanish prisoners and wounded were then transferred into a pink for return to Cuba, while *Francesa* became De Graaf's new flagship.

When news of this depredation reached Santo Domingo, the out-

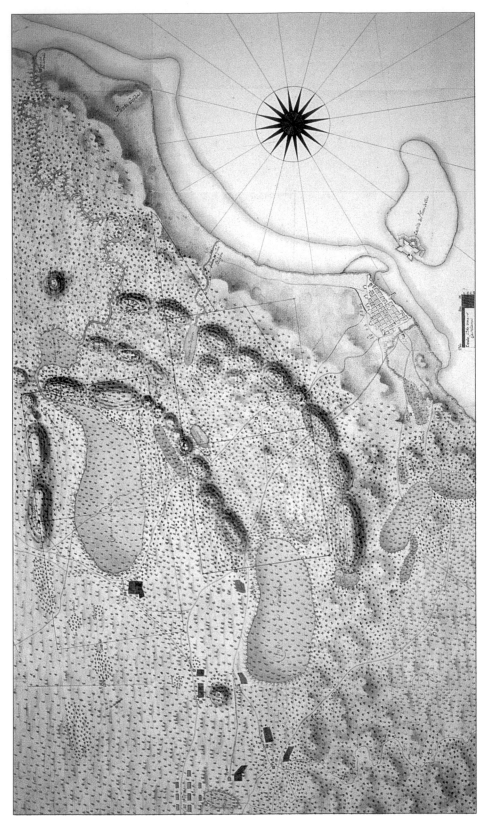

Left: Ancient map of Veracruz and its adjacent coastline. The raiders landed undetected at the headland (top left) north-northwest of this city, approaching unseen under cover of darkness to slip over its walls. (Archivo General de la Nación, Mexico)

his empty 40-gun, 400-ton ship *Saint Nicholas* (a former British slaver named *Mary and Martha*, which he had stolen from her owners), and in February 1683 obtained a letter of reprisal from the French Governor of Petit-Goâve to exact vengeance against the Spanish. To further this aim, Pouançay also put Van Hoorn in touch with the idle Grammont, whose followers soon swelled the Dutchman's depleted crew of twenty men to more than three hundred.

Determined to inflict as much punishment upon the Spaniards as possible, Van Hoorn and Grammont quit Petit-Goâve with several smaller auxiliaries, planning to attack the rich port of Veracruz, a large and tempting target which had not been assaulted in more than a century. Realising that they would need more freebooters for such a daunting task, they first steered towards Jamaica, and then the pirate haunts off the Central American coast, in expectation of uniting with the seasoned De Graaf and his Dutch confederate Michiel Andrieszoon, who were both reputedly lying there with 'two great ships, a bark, a sloop and 500 men.'

Indeed, they found these two at Roatan, and on 7 April 1683 a huge gathering of pirates met on its beach, to hear Van Hoorn and Grammont's proposal for the assault against Veracruz. Legend has it there was considerable hesitation among the crowd, until Grammont swayed any doubters by declaring: 'I would believe it almost impossible, except for the experience and valour of those who hear my words.' Inflamed, the freebooters endorsed

raged local Spaniards retaliated by expropriating a consignment of slaves brought into that port by Nikolaas van Hoorn, simply because he happened to be another Dutch adventurer with French ties. Furious at this unfair treatment, Van Hoorn in turn escaped impoundment with

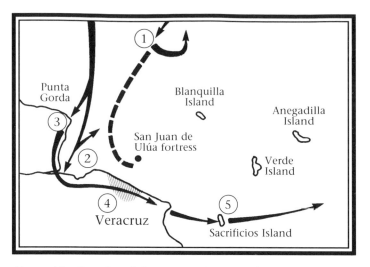

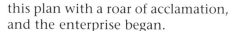

Above: De Graaf and Grammont's Sack of Veracruz (May 1683):
The pirates first reconnoitred their target (1), masquerading two scout ships as Spanish merchantmen hesitant to enter its channel (broken line) and moor opposite San Juan de Ulúa. That night they circled round and De Graaf brought two hundred men ashore near the Vergara River (2), while Grammont and Van Hoorn landed another six hundred at Punta Gorda (3). Infiltrating the city (4), they surprised its inhabitants at dawn, then after four days' pillage withdrew with four thousand captives to Sacrificios Island (5), to await ransoms.

this plan with a roar of acclamation, and the enterprise began.

Although Van Hoorn nominally occupied the position of commander-in-chief because of Pouançay's commission, actual leadership was exercised by the veterans De Graaf and Grammont, backed by their huge loyal followings. After pausing at Guanaja Island to raise even more men – among them the Jamaican George Spurre and Virginian Jacob Hall – a pirate fleet of five ships and eight lesser craft stood into the Gulf of Mexico, bearing some 1,300–1,400 raiders. With great skill, De Graaf led the way in two captured Spanish ships, hurrying to ensure that word of their design did not reach enemy ears before them.

On the afternoon of 17 May 1683, De Graaf's two advance scouts approached Veracruz alone, then broke off after closing to within ten miles and determining that the annual plate fleet had not

yet arrived. The port's lookouts assumed this pair of Spanish-built craft were friendly merchantmen afraid to attempt its shoals after dark, intending instead to enter the port next morning.

Under cover of darkness, De Graaf cunningly piloted his two vessels close inshore and landed a vanguard of two hundred buccaneers, whom he led on a reconnaissance of the sleeping city while Grammont and Van Hoorn brought another six hundred ashore farther away, and stealthily marched to join him. Veracruz had six thousand inhabitants, of whom three hundred were regular troops and another four hundred civilian militia; there were an additional three hundred soldiers occupying the outlying island fortress of San Juan de Ulúa, but the city's landward stockades were low and neglected, with sand dunes drifted up against them, so that the pirates had no difficulty stealing over these in the

moonlight and taking up position within the silent streets.

At dawn on the 18th they attacked, firing indiscriminately at every window or doorway so as to stampede the defenders. Within half an hour Veracruz was theirs, several thousand terrified, half-dressed captives being herded into the principal church. The city was then thoroughly ransacked during the next four days, and numerous prisoners tortured to reveal their hidden treasures. Grammont organised mounted companies from the stables, and De Graaf culminated this bold operation by marching the bulk of the captives down the coast and transferring them two miles offshore to Sacrificios Island, beyond any hope of rescue by Spanish relief columns. There the pirates leisurely began dividing their booty and loading up their ships, while awaiting payment of a final hostage ransom out of Mexico's interior.

Despite the atrocities committed, the Spaniards still regarded De Graaf as the more humane of the buccaneer commanders, which was confirmed by an unusual incident that occurred on Sacrificios Island. Van Hoorn, impatient because the promised ransom was slow in arriving, decided to send a dozen captives' heads ashore to hasten matters. According to Spaniards who were present, De Graaf arrived from his flagship in the nick of time to prevent this barbarity, and when his countryman rounded upon him wrathfully with drawn blade, De Graaf wounded Van Hoorn and sent him aboard *Francesa* in chains.

Shortly thereafter the ransom was received, and after herding 1,500 black and mulatto prisoners aboard

Left: Assault on a Spanish-American city.

Below: Seventeenth-century torment by thumbscrew.

as slaves, the pirate fleet weighed. They encountered the annual plate fleet just as they were standing out from the coast, but its commander, Admiral Diego Fernández de Zaldívar, deferred combat, so the raiders escaped scot-free. 'They sailed off mocking us,' one broken-hearted Spaniard lamented, 'triumphant and powerful, having lost all respect for Catholic arms.'

Ironically, Van Hoorn was to prove one of the few pirate fatalities from this venture, dying off Isla Mujeres when his wound became infected. Grammont returned to Petit-Goâve with the heavily laden *Saint Nicholas* (which he was soon to appropriate as his flagship and rename *Hardi* or 'Bold'), while De Graaf and his followers disposed of their ill-gotten booty in the maze of islands off Cuba's southern coast, then smuggled the profits into Jamaica.

Shortly afterwards, the ever restless De Graaf and his cohorts

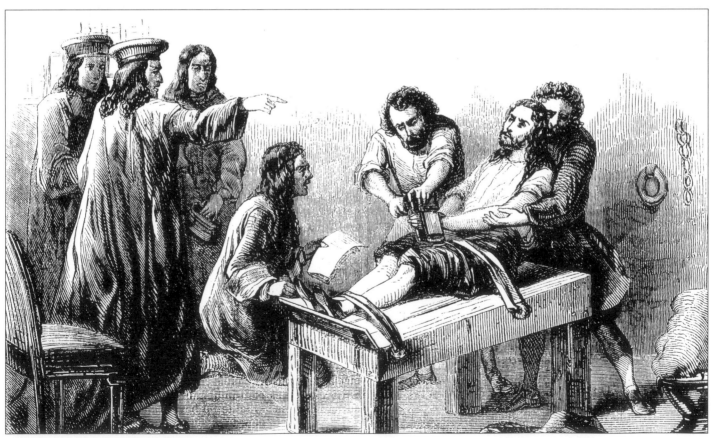

Above: Seventeenth-century corvette. Prior to going aboard Van Hoorn's *Saint Nicholas*, Grammont had a corvette such as this one, named the *Colbert*.

Left: Looters ransacking a house.

Opposite page: Man being tortured by being suspended from hands tied behind his back. A common seventeenth-century military punishment, this brutal expedient was resorted to by De Graaf and Grammont to extort money from the terrified Spanish captives in the main square of Veracruz.

Andrieszoon, Dutch-born Jan Willems, the Frenchman François Le Sage and several other lieutenants, made for the Main, arriving near Cartagena in late November 1683. When the local Governor, Juan de Pando Estrada, learnt that these pirates had arrived before his harbour, he commandeered the private ships *San Francisco* of 40 guns, *Paz* of 34, and a 28-gun galliot to chase them away. This trio sailed on 23 December 1683, manned by eight hundred sailors and soldiers under the command of Captain Andrés de Pez. But the result was scarcely as the Governor had envisaged, for the seven smaller pirate ships swarmed pugnaciously around the larger Spanish vessels, until in the confusion *San Francisco* ran aground. *Paz* struck after four hours' feverish combat, and Willems took the galliot.

Ninety Spaniards had been killed in this unexpected setback, as opposed to only twenty pirates. De

Graaf then gleefully refloated *San Francisco* to use as his new flagship, renaming her *Fortune* [later *Neptune*]; Andrieszoon received the *Paz*, naming her *Mutine* ('Rascal'); while Willems was given De Graaf's old *Francesa* or *Dauphine*. On 25 December the triumphant buccaneers deposited their Spanish prisoners ashore, with a mocking message to Cartagena's Governor, thanking him for the Christmas presents.

After a brief blockade, the pirates sailed north-westwards at the end of January 1684. *En route* De Graaf spotted a 14-gun Spanish vessel and another ship, which he deftly followed from a great distance until nightfall. Under cloak of darkness, he closed and boarded the Spaniard, seizing her with only two shots being fired, and finding her laden with 'quinine and 47 pounds of gold'. Next morning he took her consort as well, discovering her to be a British ship which the Spanish captain had captured and was carry-

ing into Cuba. De Graaf magnanimously restored this vessel to its crew, and shortly afterwards intercepted a Spanish dispatch-vessel off the southern coast of Cuba, bearing news of renewed fighting between Spain and France back in Europe (at least partly as a consequence of his own destructive raid against Veracruz).

De Graaf therefore left his confederates Andrieszoon and Willems to blockade Cuba with the other ships, while he sailed his 14-gun Spanish prize into Petit-Goâve to dispose of her cargo, and officially offer his services to the French Crown for the first time. He was made most welcome by that colony's new Governor, Pierre-Paul Tarin de Cussy, who continued his predecessor's policy of favouring privateers, and even granted this Dutch rover a *brevet de grâce* or honorary commission as an officer in Saint-Domingue's militia. De Graaf did not quit Petit-Goâve again until

His fame naturally ensured plenty of willing spirits, and a vast reunion was held on Cuba's Pinos Island in April 1685, attended by such peers as Grammont, Willems and perhaps as many as twenty other captains. This pirate assembly was so intimidating that it even cowed Captain David Mitchell, commander of the largest Royal Naval warship in the West Indies, when he chanced upon it with his 48-gun frigate *Ruby*. Going aboard Grammont's flagship, Mitchell asked that a Jamaican renegade named George Bannister be arrested for forming part of this expedition with his 36-gun *Golden Fleece*, it still being illegal for British subjects to operate under foreign commission; but the *flibustier* chieftain piously insisted that Bannister had not actually entered French service, and so Mitchell wisely 'thought it best not to insist further'.

However, De Graaf was disappointed when this huge mob unimaginatively demanded to be led on a repeat assault against Veracruz, despite his patient explanations that this city would not be caught napping a second time. Finally, in frustration he sailed for the Mosquito Coast where he was overtaken by Grammont and the others, and it was eventually decided to make a descent on the smaller Mexican port of Campeche. The pirates then shifted to Isla Mujeres to begin mustering strength.

Compared with two years earlier, this attack was a clumsy affair, with the over-confident buccaneers maintaining spotter vessels off Cape Catoche for more than a month, advising passing freebooters of their scheme, but also forewarning the Spaniards by their very presence in that region. Their preparations became so notorious that the Deputy Governor of Campeche, Felipe de la Barrera y Villegas, even had time to dispatch lookouts and spyboats up the coast to give

22 November 1684, when he set sail for the Spanish Main. (Among his 120-man crew was a new recruit, Ravenau de Lussan, who has left an interesting record of this voyage.)

On 18 January 1685 De Graaf came upon his ships *Neptune* and *Mutine* off the South American coast, operating under Andrieszoon together with four lesser buccaneer craft. After vainly maintaining watch for potential prizes off Cape de la Vela (in present-day Colom-

bia), on 8 February the pirates decided to split up. De Graaf had hoped to organise yet another major land operation such as his Veracruz raid, but not everyone in this flotilla agreed. Thus the freebooters redistributed themselves around the vessels in true Brotherhood fashion, De Graaf allowing one group to sail away with his 14-gun prize. Meanwhile he laid a course for the Gulf of Honduras in *Neptune*, hoping to recruit more followers for his scheme.

De Graaf and Grammont's Sack of Campeche (Summer 1685):
On the afternoon of 6 July 1685, more than thirty pirate sail appeared and sent boats in toward Beque (1). Spanish troops foiled this initial disembarkation, but next morning the buccaneer boats feinted a retreat toward their ships, only to then rush the nearby beach (2) and disgorge seven hundred men. De Graaf led the main body directly into the city centre (3), while Grammont mounted an encircling manoeuvre (4). Five days later a relief force of Yucatan militia arrived and was defeated (5), leaving Campeche entirely in buccaneer hands.

Grammont then organized flying columns of mounted buccaneers, who penetrated as far as 25 miles inland before finally being checked by the Spaniards at Hampolol (6). Despite this victory, the Spanish refused to advance from their base camp of Tenabó (7) until the invaders had evacuated Campeche in early September.

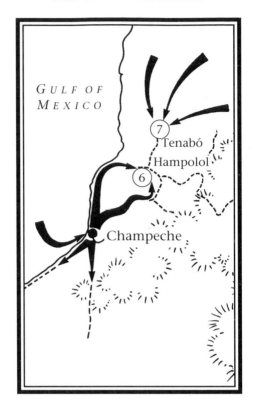

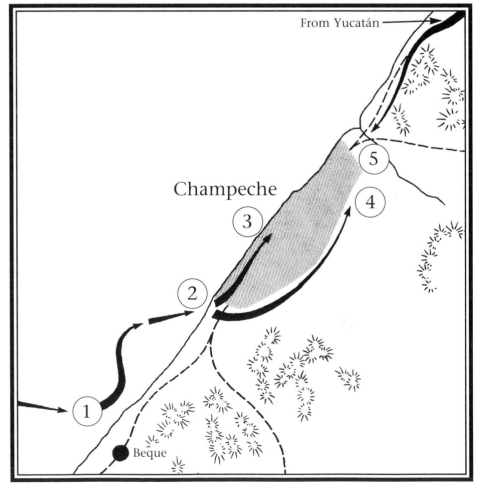

advance warning of their final approach. In late June 1685, a steady stream of reports began reaching this Spanish official of unidentified vessels creeping ever closer to his port, so that he ordered the evacuation of civilians and all their valuables.

Finally, in broad daylight on the afternoon of 6 July 1685, the dread pirate fleet appeared half a dozen miles off Campeche, comprised of six large and four small ships, six sloops, and seventeen *piraguas*. A landing force of seven hundred buccaneers immediately took to their boats and began rowing in towards shore, but the garrison was well prepared: four militia companies totalling roughly two hundred men left the city and positioned themselves opposite the raiders' intended disembarkation point. The pirates put up their helms in hesitation, not wishing to wade ashore directly into the muzzles of Spanish infantry. All night they remained bobbing on the swell, until next morning they began to draw off towards their ships, which were standing in to meet them.

But this manoeuvre proved to be a feint, and before the Spanish defenders could react, the boats rushed straight for the city, and buccaneers came swarming ashore at its very outskirts. A hundred formed up behind Capitaine Rettechard as the vanguard; two hundred joined De Graaf and marched straight towards the city centre; another two hundred advanced under Capitaine Foccard along a street parallel to De Graaf's; and the final two hundred followed Grammont in an encircling movement.

Off balance, the Spaniards fell back, while out in the harbour Captain Cristóbal Martínez de Acevedo prepared to scuttle his coastguard frigate *Nuestra Señora de la Soledad* ('Our Lady of Solitude'), in accordance with the Governor's instructions. Originally he had intended

Illac *inv. et del.*

Nous marchames tous en ligne, les prisonni
et les bagages au milieu de nous.
Relation du Capitaine bordelais Massertie

Above: *Flibustiers* evacuate a Spanish-American town, with captives and booty in their midst.

siege guns ashore from their ships and began bombarding this fortress at dawn on 12 July 1685, but at 10 o'clock they were interrupted when two relief columns of Spanish militia appeared on the beach, having hastened down from the provincial capital of Mérida de Yucatán. In the past, such troops simply had to appear for smaller raiding bands to scuttle back out to sea; but this time, the powerful freebooter host was prepared to stand and fight from behind Campeche's ramparts, so that the first ranks of Spaniards went down to unexpectedly well-aimed volleys.

All day the battle raged back and forth, until Grammont circled behind the Spanish militiamen and caught them between two fires. The relief force then broke up and withdrew in disarray, while that night Campeche's beleaguered garrison also mutinied. Their officers begged these men to remain at their posts until daybreak when they might seek terms, but the soldiers replied 'pirates keep faith with no one', and threatened to shoot any officer who got in their way. By 11 pm the citadel was deserted, and a couple of English prisoners who had been held within its dungeons shouted these tidings to the besiegers. These called back for the fort's artillery to be discharged, so that the buccaneers might advance knowing the guns to be empty. Once this was done, they poured exultantly over the walls, led by De Graaf and Grammont in person.

But the conquerors' joy soon turned to bitterness when they gradually discovered that most of the city's wealth had been withdrawn into the interior, because of the ample warnings received prior to their assault. Captives were threatened with terrible punishment if ransoms were not forthcoming, but Yucatán's Governor, Juan Bruno Téllez de Guzmán, had strictly prohibited any such pay-

merely to bore holes in her bottom and thus prevent her falling into enemy hands, but given the rapidity of the invaders' advance, he now directed his boatswain to run a trail of powder into the magazine. From the frigate's launch Martínez lit the fuse, and *Soledad* exploded with such a startling blast that it put paid

to the remaining shreds of the defenders' morale, and sent them scurrying into the safety of their citadel while the pirates entered Campeche unopposed.

Over the next few days the invaders subdued other isolated strongpoints within the city – including the cathedral, whose refugees managed to escape through an ancient tunnel leading outside the city walls – until eventually only the citadel remained. The pirates then manhandled heavy

The French chieftain then further delayed weighing because a fair number of his contingent were ashore at two small chapels, so that his ship fell behind as its British consorts emerged to engage the enemy force.

This proved to be the Armada del Mar del Sur (literally, the 'South Sea Fleet'), the Spanish squadron normally stationed at Callao, Peru, which had sailed that previous month under its Lieutenant-General Tomás Palavacino. His command consisted of the 40-gun flagship *San José*, with a crew of 405 men; the 36-gun vice-flagship *Nuestra Señora de Guadalupe*, with 374 men; the 26-gun frigate *San Lorenzo*; the hired merchantmen *Nuestra Señora del Pópulo* and *Nuestra Señora del Rosario*, mounting 20 guns apiece; plus a 6-gun tender and 6-gun fireship. In all, this force comprised 1,431 Spaniards, none of whom had any previous combat experience at sea.

The action commenced as a tentative, long-range bombardment, with both Davis and Swan unwilling to close with the more powerful Armada vessels, who in turn feared being outmanoeuvred, separated and then boarded by their more ferocious opponents. Thus all that afternoon the two formations wheeled around each other in the Gulf of Panama, firing ineffectually at long range until darkness fell. During that night Palavacino made use of a stratagem of extinguishing and rekindling lights on his ships, which deceived the buccaneers into believing he had shifted position.

Instead the Spanish ships were still in good order next morning, while it was the pirates who were now further scattered, and their attempts to regroup turned into a rout. The day ended with a Spanish victory, as the divided raiders were driven off westward towards Coiba Island, and the blockade of Panama was broken. Nevertheless the Armada had failed to make any captures, so that the buccaneers' strength remained unimpaired, while the Spaniards soon after lost their capital ship *San José* to an accidental fire and explosion, while anchored off Paita on 5 September 1685. This blast killed 241 of the South Americans' most able officers and sailors, and cost them irreplaceable artillery pieces and accoutrements, which Peru's impoverished treasury could not easily replace.

In the meantime the dejected buccaneers had fallen out among themselves along national lines, each group blaming the other for this defeat. A failed attack on the coastal town of Remedios followed at the beginning of July, after which both contingents headed north-westward as separate formations. Davis, Swan, Townley and Knight raided Realejo and León (Nicaragua) in early August 1685, but for little gain. Grogniet and his *flibustiers* had refused to join in either of these operations, the French commander preferring to take 120 of his men in five boats for a repeat attempt against Remedios. This assault was repulsed and he rejoined his remaining two hundred *flibustiers* aboard *Santa Rosa* on 3 September. The French then entered Realejo on 1 November, but naturally found it devastated from the earlier British assault, so obtained no booty.

Meanwhile Davis and Knight had shifted southward with two other vessels, while Swan and Townley continued farther north towards Mexico, hoping to intercept the annual galleon arriving across the Pacific from Manila in the Philippines. Grogniet and his French contingent therefore remained alone off the Central American coast, at first hesitating, but then marching inland to attack Esparta (Costa Rica) on 9 December, then pressing on into the Gulf of Chiriquí toward the end of the year. On 9 January 1686 his *flibustiers* captured the tiny coastal town of Chiriquita (Panama), which they abandoned a week later.

At the end of this same month a Spanish squadron passed them out at sea, so that when Grogniet's men approached Remedios again on the night of 5/6 March to forage for supplies, they were ambushed by a small frigate, *barco luengo* and *piragua*, which inflicted more than thirty casualties. Driven westward by this setback, the French pirates anchored off Esparto on the 19th, then four days later sighted Townley's small flotilla again.

Despite some residual ill will between the two formations, the British and French buccaneers agreed to combine for a joint attempt against the inland city of Granada (Nicaragua), landing a force of 345 men on 7 April under Grogniet, Rose and Townley, which fought its way into that city three days later. Once again, though, little loot was found, as the Spaniards had been forewarned and withdrawn their valuables to Zapatera Island, so that the pirates retired empty-handed five days later.

They endured numerous ambuscades on their way back to the ships, including a major action near the town of Masaya, where they found five hundred militia barring their path. The marauders easily shot their way through, scattering the inexperienced, poorly armed Nicaraguan militiamen, after which they regained the coast and sailed away together for Realejo.

But having enjoyed such limited success so far, half of Grogniet's followers voted on 9 June 1686 to for-sake their French leader in favour of Townley, joining him in his proposed eastward progression towards Panama. The remaining 148 *flibustiers* agreed to remain with Grogniet while he sailed away in the opposite direction, and the two contingents parted company a fortnight later.

Grogniet operated for a time in the 'Gulf of Amapala' (today's Gulf of Fonseca), until a majority of his men again voted to quit his command. This latter band, comprised of 85 *flibustiers*, sailed *Santa Rosa* north-westward towards Mexico and California, intending to waylay the Philippine galleon (which had eluded Swan that previous winter, leading him to strike out in frustration across the Pacific, following in that vessel's wake towards Guam and the East Indies).

Meanwhile Grogniet retraced his course down the Central American coast with 60 loyal hands, aboard three *piraguas*. On 23 January 1687 he rediscovered Townley's contingent in the Gulf of Nicoya, now commanded by one George Hout (or Hutt). After parting company from the French commander, Townley had made a sudden descent on the outskirts of Panama on 22 July 1686, seizing merchandise estimated to be worth one and a half million pesos, but subsequently losing this in a Spanish counter-ambush. None the less Townley had made off with fifteen thousand pesos in silver and almost three hundred captives, which he had then used to brutally secure a truce. Sending two captives' heads to the President of the Audiencia of Panama, he had forced this official to supply the pirates with cattle, sheep and flour on a daily basis. Meanwhile, Townley had also threatened to send another 50 heads ashore if five buccaneers in Spanish hands were not released.

After a month of this uneasy relationship, the Spaniards attempted a surprise attack on 22 August 1686, slipping a force of three ships and 240 men out of Perico Island to fall upon the idle raiders. This assault had been fiercely beaten off, two of the Spanish ships being captured, and only 65 Spaniards emerging uninjured from this fight. Townley himself had been wounded during the battle, which prompted him to wrathfully send another twenty heads ashore in protest against this violation of the truce. The Spanish had responded by delivering an additional ten thousand pesos to him on 4 September, together with a conciliatory note from the Archbishop of Panama saying that all English prisoners would henceforth be considered as Catholics, and as such entitled to the protection of the Church.

But Townley had not been able to savour this victory for long, as four days later he had died of his wounds. His body had been cast overboard – in accordance with his

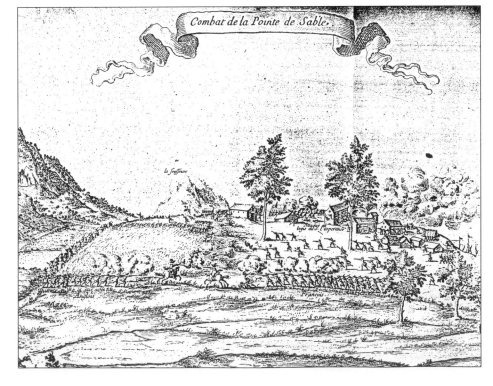

Left: Ambush of Swan's foraging party near Sentispac, Mexico, February 1686, in which Basil Ringrose and another fifty buccaneers died.

PORTVS ACAPVLCO

Previous spread: Nocturnal embarkation. (National Maritime Museum, Greenwich)

Above: Imaginary view of the port of Acapulco during the seventeenth century, with Mexican merchants arriving to meet the annual galleon from Manila.

wishes – near Otoque Island, and Hout had assumed overall command of his force. Once reunited with Grogniet, these two groups then continued to ravage that area for another month, before finally weighing to shift their operations farther south. It was their intention to arrive off the South American coast and surprise the Ecuadorian port of Guayaquil.

On 16 April they appeared opposite Puná Island, and two hours before dawn on Sunday the 20th landed a force to begin marching inland. Grogniet led his company through a marsh directly towards the heart of Guayaquil, while Hout advanced against one small fort guarding its approaches, and Picard directed his men against another. The Spaniards had earlier been advised of strange sails off Puná, but when no attack had immediately developed, assumed this to be a false alarm.

Early on that rainy Sunday morning they were disabused, when the buccaneers burst upon their city unexpectedly and launched into a vicious house-to-house contest. From 34 to 60 Spaniards were killed in the eight hours of fighting that ensued, and many others captured, as opposed to only nine pirate dead and a dozen wounded. But among the latter figured Grogniet, who was carried back aboard his flagship when the triumphant raiders evacuated Guayaquil four days later. He died of his wounds on 2 May off Puná, while still awaiting the ransom of the Spanish hostages.

Picard now assumed overall command of the French *flibustiers*, who together with Hout were joined a few days later by Davis. The latter had been raiding along the South American coast with Knight, but brought word that a squadron of Peruvian privateers was presently on its way to attack the Guayaquil raiders. These interceptors actually hove into view on 27 May, consisting of the purchased vessels *San José* and *San Nicolás* of 20 guns apiece, commanded by the Biscayans Dionisio López de Artunduaga and Nicolás de Igarza respectively, plus a small *patache*. The pirate formation included almost twenty medium and small-size craft, mostly prizes, which the Peruvian privateers rather gingerly engaged.

As at Pacheca Island, a long-range gun duel ensued over the next five days, with the Spaniards eventually scattering the raiders and recovering some of their vessels. During this action *San Nicolás* ran hard aground on a sand bank off Atacames, and limped back into Callao making water. She was quickly replaced by *San Francisco de Paula* and another *patache*, which joined López de Artunduaga off Ecuador and resumed the long-distance pursuit of the retreating buccaneers. Although undefeated, Picard, Davis and their consorts were forced to abandon their largest prize, *San Jacinto*, and ten days later held a meeting at Cape San Francisco where they agreed on a final division of spoils.

Each then went his separate way, Picard sailing with five vessels as far north as Tehuantepec (Mexico), which he captured with 180 men on 30 August 1687, before looking into Acapulco Bay a few weeks later. Reversing course until he had reached the Gulf of Fonseca, Picard scuttled his vessels on 2 January 1688, after again fending off the Peruvian privateers.

In a singularly bold move, he next marched deep into Nueva Segovia province with 260 followers, determined to fight his way through the heart of Central America until he reached the West Indies. Penetrating as far as the interior highlands, his buccaneers discovered the Coco River and built a number of rafts on which they sped down its waterways, until they emerged exultantly at Cape Gracias a Dios – more than three hundred miles away – on 9 March. A passing Jamaican ship was then persuaded to carry them to Saint-Domingue, which they reached on 8 April.

Like Sharpe and the other South Sea raiders before him, Picard and his *flibustiers* remained leery of official sanction, because they knew full well that peace had long since been restored between France and Spain (although they feigned ignorance of this because of their lengthy absence). They were fortunate in that Governor de Cussy was

Below: Crude engraving of a West Indian *piragua*, being an undecked vessel propelled by both sails and oars.

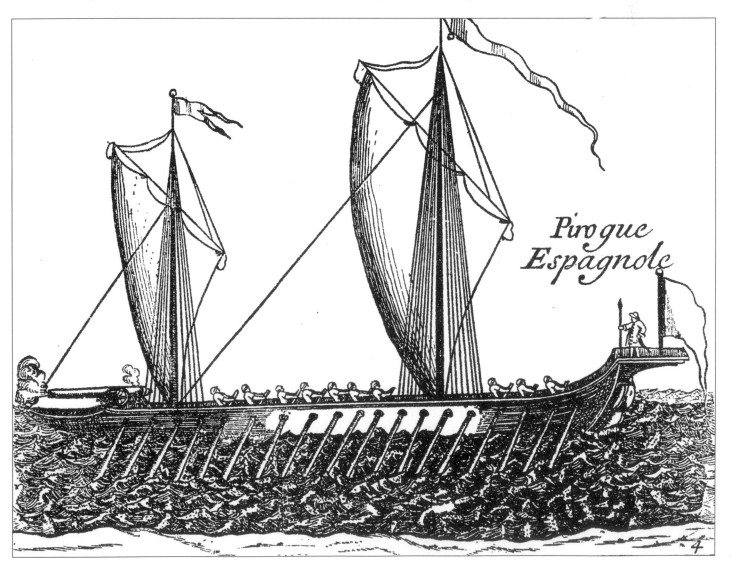

Pirogue Espagnole

Right: Seventeenth-century French privateer captain.

not present in his capital of Petit-Goâve at that moment, being on an inspection tour of the island's northern districts, so the renegades received no reproof. Nevertheless it became quite obvious to them that France's policy had changed drastically with regards to West Indian roving, despite the local Crown officers' continual distrust of their Spanish-American neighbours. So Picard and many other freebooters decided to disperse even farther afield, emigrating to French North America or France to enjoy their spoils.

Much the same reaction awaited their British colleagues. After parting company at Cape San Francisco, Davis had proceeded southward and eventually followed Sharpe and Knight's route out of the South Pacific, by exiting via the Straits of Magellan. Touching briefly at the River Plate, he then rounded Brazil and headed into the Caribbean, leery as to what his reception might be. Meeting up with a Barbados sloop commanded by one Edwin Carter, Davis and his marauders learnt of King James II's recent 'proclamation to pardon and call in the buccaneers' (most probably that of 22 May 1687 Old Style), and so decided to sail with Carter's sloop all the way to Philadelphia – well removed from the West Indian arena of operations – where they arrived in May 1688.

After a brief stay, during which they hurriedly secured pardons from the local Crown authorities, Davis, Lionel Wafer and a few other rovers travelled to their former sanctuary of Virginia, hoping to disappear back into civilian life. But on their arrival in June 1688, they were immediately arrested by Captain Simon Rowe of HMS *Dumbarton* on the suspicion of piracy, because of the £1,500 worth of battered silver

they carried with them. Davis and his companions insisted that this had been procured in the South Seas merely to help them 'spend the remainder of their days honestly and quietly', yet they were put in irons. When Rowe further questioned a black slave they had brought with them from the Pacific, he came to the conclusion that the rovers should have been hanged

many times over as multiple murderers.

But instead Davis and the rest of his men were deported to stand trial in England, being allowed to travel freely aboard the merchantman *Effingham* in late 1690, their good behaviour guaranteed by dispatching their treasure-trove aboard another vessel. Eventually, after a lengthy proceeding, Davis and the

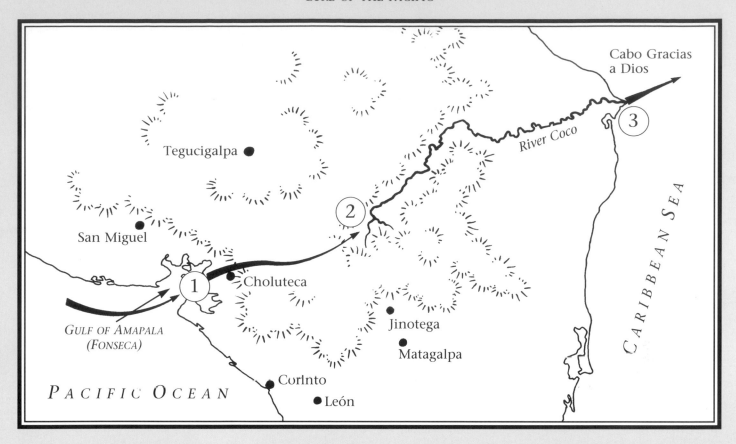

others were cleared, although forced to cede £300 of their booty towards the establishment of a new centre of studies in Virginia, which became the College of William and Mary. By this late date the South Sea had largely become devoid of buccaneer intruders, the sole exception being the vessel of Capitaine Franco, a latecomer to this particular campaigning.

He had originally set sail from New England towards the Guinea Coast (West Africa), whence he departed again on 11 December 1686 to join the privateering forces known to be still operating in the Pacific. Franco was later described in Spanish records as possibly Dutch – his name may have been Frank or Frankel – although serving under a French commission. His small ship had entered the Straits of Magellan in early March 1687, emerging one month later into the South Pacific. By 27 June he was off the Gulf of Guayaquil, after which he touched at Coiba Island on 20

July, before entering the Gulf of Panama on 4 August. Here, discovering that the *flibustiers* he had hoped to meet were already being driven out of those waters, he decided to proceed even further north-westward – despite having only 41 crew-members – to prowl the coast of New Spain.

Franco may have been the rover who landed at Acaponeta (Mexico) more than a year later, on 14 November 1688, carrying off 'forty women, much silver and people', including a Jesuit priest and a Mercedarian friar. This same intruder was also chased away by ships from Acapulco early next year, who described his vessel as being 'old and with few people on it'.

By June 1689 Franco had returned to South America, and shortly thereafter visited the remote Galàpagos Islands, which he was to turn into a base. His numbers proved insufficient for any land raids, however, as was revealed when Franco captured the ship *San*

Above: Picard's Fighting Retreat from the Pacific (1688):
On 2 January 1688, after skirmishing with some Peruvian privateers in the Gulf of Fonseca (1), Picard scuttled his ships and led 260 followers inland, hoping to regain the West Indies. The local Spaniards allowed his small army past Choluteca into the central highlands, where Picard found the head-waters of the Coco River (2). Constructing rafts, he headed downstream to emerge at Cape Gracias a Dios (3) by March 9th, from whence he commandeered a Jamaican ship to carry him on to Saint-Domingue.

Francisco Xavier out of Puná on 15 October 1689, and the Spanish captives later reported that he had only a total of 89 men on board: 34 of them French, four Dutch, an English pilot, and the rest Latin-American blacks or Indians.

Despite his meagre complement, Franco continued to ply the South Seas for another four years,

notwithstanding every Spanish attempt to drive him out, and even succeeded in rounding the Horn and returning to Europe safely at the end of this period. However, he was never joined in the Pacific by any more West Indian buccaneers from across the Isthmus, as had so often happened before. The reason for this was that these men were otherwise distracted, by that cruel sport called war.

Above: Woodes Rogers's privateers search the *señoritas* of Guayaquil, Ecuador, in 1709. His circumnavigation was inspired by the Pacific exploits of earlier buccaneers.

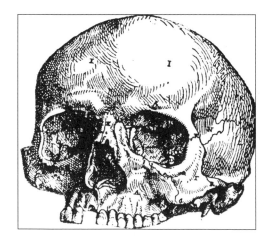

VII

The Last Buccaneer Armies

Ye gallants all, take heed how you
Come to untimely ends;
Justice has bid the world adieu,
And dead men have no friends.
Sir Charles Sedley (1639–1701)

The War of the League of Augsburg (which would become known in America as 'King William's War,' and later as the Nine Years War) had gradually evolved from frictions back in Europe. Slowly, a broad alliance had coalesced to contain the rise of France under its great 'Sun King' Louis XIV. As early as November 1688, a 42-year-old slaver and junior captain (*capitaine de frégate*) in the French royal navy named Jean-Baptiste Ducasse had led an unsuccessful assault against the Dutch colony of Suriname, on the Wild Coast of South America.

But fighting only truly exploded in the spring of the following year, when France attempted to reverse England's 'Glorious Revolution', in which the pro-Catholic James II had been deposed in favour of the Protestant Dutch rulers, William and Mary. The French thus found themselves ranged in a war against the combined might of England, Holland and Spain, as well as several lesser powers on the Continent. Such a development seemed to hold out the promise of ample employment for West Indian privateers.

And indeed, the initial round of hostilities in the New World erupted around the Lesser Antilles, which were always the first to receive any news speeding across the Atlantic. Governor-General Charles de Courbon, comte de

Right: A French man-of-war leaves its Spanish opponent ablaze, during the opening phases of the War of the League of Augsburg.

Return of a Spanish expedition.
(National Maritime Museum,
Greenwich)

Blénac, quickly mustered a force of six warships, fourteen merchantmen and twenty-three island sloops at Martinique, which he led in attacks against the British portion of the island of Saint Christopher (St Kitts, still shared between France and England), as well as Dutch Sint Eustatius. Among his following was the recently promoted Ducasse, in command of a contingent of 120 *flibustiers*.

Blénac's expedition arrived off Basseterre, Saint Christopher, on 27 July 1689, his troops dashing ashore and laying 'the southern part of the island in ashes', according to one eye-witness. Worse still, the British leader Colonel Thomas Hill and 400–500 of his followers were driven into the tiny confines of Fort Charles at Old Road Town, where they became besieged. Blénac cautiously dug an approach trench

while his batteries and warships bombarded its gate from long range, although the fortress itself had no moat, and only gently sloping walls to protect the outnumbered defenders.

More importantly, a hill overlooked its interior, and after two weeks' fruitless firing Ducasse finally persuaded the Governor-General that a battery might better be installed atop that prominence. Blénac reluctantly agreed, and during the night of 14/15 August Ducasse's buccaneers dragged six heavy artillery pieces to its crest. The following morning they opened fire, and the besieged Englishmen surrendered once they found their counter-fire could not reach this summit, so that the entire island passed into French hands.

Despite this opening-round success, Blénac's fortunes soon

reversed, as British volunteers and privateers began pouring in from throughout the Caribbean. One of the first to respond was Thomas Hewetson, a commander who had departed England more than a year earlier with a small peacetime flotilla, intent on following the buccaneers' old route into the South Pacific and founding an intruder settlement in Chile.

Instead, his ships had been unable to beat their way through the Straits of Magellan, so that he had retreated to Tobago with his 50-gun flagship *Lion* and two other vessels, where he further learnt that his licence from James II was no longer valid because of that monarch's deposition. As a final blow, upon reaching Barbados one of his ships exploded at anchor towards the end of July 1689, after which a discouraged Hewetson – most of his men having deserted – prepared to sail back to England as escort for a homeward-bound merchant convoy.

But when he touched at Bermuda, Hewetson discovered that hostilities had broken out back in Europe, and his luck at last improved. The local Governor, Sir Robert Robinson, furnished him with a privateering commission dated 19 October 1689, then helped him raise sufficient freebooters to bring *Lion*'s strength up to '350 lusty men'. Thus reinforced, Hewetson returned to Antigua by the middle of the following month, and offered his services to Governor Christopher Codrington of the Leeward Islands.

The latter promptly appointed him 'commander-in-chief of all vessels fitted out' in those waters, then dispatched Hewetson's flotilla of three ships and two sloops in a

Right: Jean Bart, the legendary French corsair whose career achieved its peak during the War of the League of Augsburg.

retaliatory strike against the French island of Marie Galante, with orders to 'reduce it, securing the plunder for himself and his fellow adventurers'. Among Hewetson's captains was a 44-year-old, hot-tempered Scot named William Kidd, commanding the 20-gun *Blessed William* with a crew of 80–90 men.

This small force successfully descended on the French island on 30 December 1689 (Old Style), ransacking it over the next five days, before coming away with considerable booty. On returning to Nevis, Hewetson's squadron was hurried out to sea again to rescue the expedition of Sir Thomas Thornhill,

Right: Soldier loading a musket.

which had become cut off after attacking the French colony of Saint Martin. Hewetson arrived off that island in late January 1690, to find the British troops beleaguered ashore by Ducasse, who had been rushed to his compatriots' rescue with three men-of-war, a brigantine and a sloop, landing seven hundred French reinforcements in the nick of time to reverse the tide of battle.

Presently the two squadrons confronted each other offshore, exchanging broadsides throughout much of that first day, until Ducasse withdrew at nightfall. The next day the British succeeded in driving the French even farther away, thus allowing Hewetson to bring off Thornhill's men and return to Nevis in triumph. But not every Englishman experienced this same sense of elation, as the unpaid rank-and-file buccaneers resented their involvement in a full-scale line-of-battle engagement against heavily armed men-of-war, rather than seeking out easy, rich targets for plunder.

When Kidd went ashore on 12 February 1690, his men mutinied and made off with *Blessed William*, together with their captain's £2,000 share of Marie Galante loot. Kidd set off in angry pursuit aboard another vessel, eventually reaching as far as New York City, where he married and settled down, while Hewetson soon after transferred from Nevis to Barbados, where he was issued yet another privateering commission at the end of April 1690 to protect that island as well. But when fresh reinforcements arrived from England, Hewetson too decided to seek better opportunities elsewhere, and chartered *Lion* to the factor of the Spanish slave *asiento* for a commercial voyage and departed this theatre.

The West Indian freebooters were now degenerating into an unreliable military force, at a time when professional services were growing increasingly effective. In contrast, the rovers no longer had the will nor ability to attack major enemy cities, preferring instead to operate against softer targets, mostly as commerce raiders. Gone was the brave core of soldier-colonists who had given their earlier forays such discipline and firepower; in their place were disgruntled merchant seamen and runaway landsmen intent on acquiring booty.

Most of their charismatic leaders were also either dead, such as Grammont, or retired like Morgan, while vulnerable objectives and well-protected sanctuaries were becoming ever scarcer in the Caribbean. The Anglo-Dutch alliance with Madrid further complicated matters, as it prevented the traditional co-operation between Jamaican buccaneers and Saint-Domingue *flibustiers*, which had proven so devastating in past conflicts. Furthermore, the latter soon began experiencing heavy setbacks of their own.

When informed of this latest outbreak of hostilities, Governor de Cussy had written bitterly to his superiors in Paris from Port-de-Paix on 24 August 1689: 'I destroyed privateering here because the court so willed it,' adding that if he had not done so 'there would be ten or twelve stout ships on this coast, with many brave people aboard to preserve this colony and its commerce.' Nevertheless he decided to launch a major local offensive with the few forces at his disposal. In summer he marched across the border into the interior of Spanish Santo Domingo and captured the frontier stronghold of Santiago de los Caballeros with a small army of *habitant* militia and *flibustiers*.

Wholly unexpectedly, this provoked a massive counter-strike from the Spaniards. Galvanised into action by this loss of territory, a host of Spanish volunteers mustered at the capital city of Santo Domingo by the end of 1690. When half-a-dozen vessels from the Armada de Barlovento arrived, 2,600 men trooped aboard these, while another seven hundred advanced directly across the island under Governor Francisco de Segura Sandoval. The Armada ships departed on 21 December, circling around the eastern tip while the Spanish army forced the French occupiers to relinquish Santiago, and fall back. Still more astonishingly, De Segura then pressed on until he reached the northern shores, where he rendezvoused with the Armada contingent near Manzanillo Bay and advanced deep into French territory with these reinforcements, intent on attacking the town of Cap-François (present-day Cap Haïtien).

This *quartier* or district was governed by De Graaf, who had retired from roving and been granted French citizenship, the title of *mayor*, and invested in the Order of Saint Louis. Confronted by these strangely reversed roles, in which the French were now preparing to defend their homes against Spanish raiders for the first time, an overconfident De Cussy rushed to the rescue of Cap-François. Despite

being outnumbered three-to-one, he remained sufficiently contemptuous of Spanish fighting ability to offer immediate battle at the Sabane de la Limonade just outside that town, rather than allow his enemy to penetrate further.

The two armies clashed on 21 January 1691, and at first everything seemed to go well for the better-armed French. However, at a crucial moment during the engagement a regiment of Spanish lancers rose from the tall grass and fell upon De Cussy's musketeers as they were reloading, thus engulfing them in a hand-to-hand mêlée where superior numbers could tell. The day ended with a crushing Spanish victory, almost five hundred Frenchmen being slain, includ-

ing De Cussy and most of his senior officers (except De Graaf, who fled into the nearby hills), at a cost of only 47 Spaniards dead.

The victors then rampaged exultantly throughout that district, pillaging the surrounding countryside before finally torching Cap-François and several of the vessels in its roads, and withdrawing with 130 slaves and two prizes. News of this devastating loss spread rapidly throughout the West Indies, puncturing the myth of buccaneer invincibility. Spanish morale soared, while that of the *flibustiers* sagged at seeing their home bases destroyed. Two weeks later Ducasse stepped ashore amid the burnt remains of Cap-François, visiting the nearby battlefield where he found the hor-

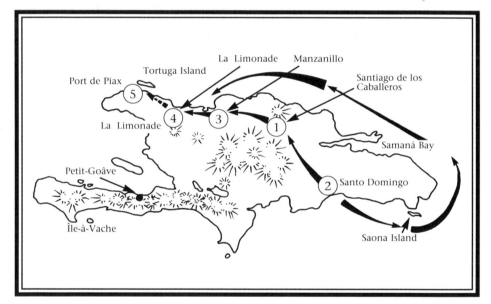

Above: Spanish Sweeps Through the Buccaneer Strongholds of Saint-Domingue (January 1691 and Spring 1695):
In July 1690, a small French army crossed the border and occupied the Spanish frontier town of Santiago de los Caballeros (1). The Spaniards retaliated five months later by sending seven hundred troops overland from Santo Domingo (2), along with another 2,600 circling round the island aboard six warships. After freeing Santiago, these two units rendezvoused at Manzanillo Bay (3), to advance together against Cap François (modern-day Cap Haïtien). The outnumbered French offered battle at Sabane de la Limonade (4), where they were massacred on 21 January 1691.

Four years later, the Spaniards again swept through the north-western corner of Saint-Domingue, this time in conjunction with an English expeditionary force under Colonel Luke Lillingston and Commodore Robert Wilmot. After landing east of Cap François in late May 1695, the invaders (broken line) rampaged as far west as Port de Paix (5), which they destroyed before withdrawing with booty and numerous captives.

Above: Hispaniola.

rifying spectacle of De Cussy's corpse and three hundred others 'not yet buried, being rotted and half desiccated'. Shortly afterwards Ducasse went to France, to report on this disaster, and at the end of March 1691 left La Rochelle for the New World again.

Upon his return to Martinique, Ducasse learned that a large British force under Royal Naval Captain Lawrence Wright had arrived in the Antilles, and in conjunction with Governor Codrington of the Leeward Islands was besieging Guadeloupe. Once more Ducasse hastened to the rescue, by conveying two companies of French infantry and six hundred *flibustiers* aboard his *Hasardeux* ('Daring'), *Mignon* ('Dainty'), *Emerillon* ('Merlin'), *Cheval Marin* ('Sea Horse') and three 20-gun merchantmen. Know-

ing himself to be heavily outnumbered, he intended to avoid combat altogether, while depositing these troops by stealth to aid the beleaguered garrison.

During his passage he also freed Marie Galante from British occupation, then began landing his reinforcements at Grosier, Guadeloupe, on 23 May 1691. Much to his surprise the British withdrew two days later, their spirits having been thoroughly sapped by torrential rains, and an enormous sick list resulting from the unhealthy climate. Wright even refused to remain offshore, much less engage Ducasse, despite his numerical advantage.

Returning to Martinique, Ducasse transferred to Saint Croix on 2 August in the hope of alleviating an outbreak of yellow fever aboard his ships, then on the 7th sailed again for Port-de-Paix on the north shore of Hispaniola, where his two warships and single corvette lost 250

men before the disease abated. He was still lying there on 1 October when a letter arrived from Paris, appointing him Governor of Saint-Domingue in succession to the dead De Cussy. He knew this island's colonists to be still shaken and confused in the wake of that spring's disaster, yet was able to restore some of their confidence through vigorous counter-measures.

When it was rumoured the Spaniards were about to invade the northern *quartiers* again that winter, Ducasse sailed from his capital of Petit-Goâve on 16 February 1692, conveying a company of militia reinforcements aboard two corsair vessels. He landed with this contingent at Port-de-Paix four days later, forwarding the *flibustier* Sieur Dumesnil and his freebooters to Cap-François to bolster the depleted local forces under De Graaf and his immediate subordinate, Charles-François Le Vasseur de Beauregard.

The expected Spanish attack never developed, however, and in the words of Ducasse: 'From the moment the *flibustiers* knew that the Spaniards' design had been aborted, they exited with five or six vessels.'

Despite his long association with such independent spirits, he found this self-centredness particularly galling in this climate of crisis. Frustrated at being deprived of desperately needed men on such a whim, the Governor added:

> They are very bad subjects, who believe they have not been put in the world except to practise brigandage and piracy. Enemies of subordination and authority, their example ruins the colonies, all the young people having no other wish than to embrace this profession for its libertinage and ability to gain booty.

Ducasse's British counterparts might have voiced similar opinions, especially as the general lack of legitimate prizes soon began tempting their own rovers into more disreputable ventures.

Britain's alliance with Spain and Holland meant that vessels from these two nations were not subject to seizure, while the relatively few French merchantmen quickly vanished from the high seas (except for well-protected convoys). Thus the large swarm of privateers found scant opportunity of gaining prize-money, and so cast about for other prey.

They soon succumbed to the allure of the Far East, which – however distant – at least offered the temptation of rich merchantmen with little military protection. Some rovers had already probed this far, following the track of the fabled East Indiamen around the Cape of Good Hope, or even travelling westward across the Pacific Ocean from Mexico. But it was not until word

began spreading of available sanctuaries on the strategically placed island of Madagascar, that large numbers of privateers forsook the war for easier campaigns in the Red Sea and Indian Ocean.

One of the first pirate settlers on this island was Adam Baldridge, a Jamaican buccaneer who had fled there as long ago as 1685, after murdering a man. He had established himself on the islet of Saint Mary's, cowing the native tribesmen with

Above: Romanticized nineteenth-century view of pirate life on Madagascar.

his musket-toting followers. This bottle-necked harbour proved to be one of the most defensible anchorages on that entire coast, and over the years Baldridge had built a castle-like mansion high atop its hill, clearly visible from out at sea and protected by a stockaded fort with forty guns, overlooking a group of warehouses. From these he traded with every passing ship, buying stolen or legitimate goods, and bartering or reselling these to pirates and honest merchants alike.

His harbour became a favourite stopping-place for Far Eastern traders, and was even celebrated in one of the popular ditties of that day:

> Where is the trader of London town?
> His gold's on the capstan,
> His blood's on his gown,
> And it's up and away for Saint Mary's Bay,
> Where the liquor is good, and the lasses are gay.

At its peak, some 1,500 Europeans inhabited Saint Mary's, and Baldridge became known as the 'King of the Pirates'.

Vessels were fitted out from as far away as New England to make this immense voyage around the Cape, first visiting the West African slave depots, then Madagascar on their outward passage, before touching in the West Indies on the homeward leg. Those who undertook its hardships became known as 'Red Seamen,' and the trip itself was often referred to as the 'Pirate Round', because of the increasing number of raiders who followed in its wake. Such forays were given even greater impetus after the destruction of Port Royal, Jamaica, by the terrible earthquake of June 1692, which further weakened the British Crown's control over their West Indian privateers.

One of the most notorious of these new adventurers began his campaign in December 1692, when the veteran Jamaican rover Thomas Tew (originally from Rhode Island) purchased a privateering commission from Lieutenant-Governor Isaac Richier of Bermuda, ostensibly to operate against the French. He then bought a partial share in and obtained command of the 70-ton

sloop *Amity* of eight guns, which the previous year had been serving out of Barbados under Captain Richard Gilbert. Tew further recruited a crew of perhaps 60 hardbitten men, with whom he set out from Bermuda in January 1693 accompanied by the sloop of yet another dishonest captain, George Dew.

These two were supposedly bound on a raid against the French slaving factory of Gorée in West

Above: Tew in conversation with New York's corrupt Governor Fletcher, as imagined by Howard Pyle.

Africa, despite their tiny numbers; but a few days out into the Atlantic Dew's sloop sprang its mast in a storm and turned back. Left alone, Tew now revealed to his ship's company that he proposed making a piratical foray into the Far East:

... a course which should lead them to ease and plenty, in which they might pass the rest of their days. That one bold push would do their business, and they might return home, not only without danger, but even with reputation. The crew finding he expected their resolution, cried out, one and all: 'A gold chain, or a wooden leg, we'll stand by you!'

Tew and his men altered course to round the Cape, emerging after a lengthy passage into the Arabian Sea.

Several weeks' unavailing search ensued, until Tew intercepted an immensely rich merchant vessel belonging to the Great Moghul of India. His heavily armed freebooters easily subdued the Indian troops guarding this ship, and carried it by storm after a one-sided fusillade in which they suffered not a single loss. Tew then sailed his ill-gotten prize to Baldridge's bolthole of Saint Mary's, where he divided the spoils and safely careened his ship. By December 1693 all was ready, and *Amity* once again set sail for the New World.

Crossing the Atlantic, Tew deliberately bypassed Bermuda in favour of his home port of Newport, Rhode Island, where he arrived in April 1694, after logging more than 22,000 sea miles during his epic fifteen-month cruise. The local citizenry were dazzled by his exploit, especially when they beheld the exotic assortment of plunder he brought in: gold, silver, jewellery, elephants' tusks, ivory, spices and silk, the whole valued at more than £100,000. Tew's seamen received shares ranging from £1,200 to an astonishing £3,000 apiece, and the formerly inconsequential captain now found himself a rich man.

He was accorded a hero's welcome by the townsfolk, most of whom turned a blind eye to the criminal nature of his enterprise. One of the few exceptions was John Easton, the honest Quaker Governor, who when Tew approached him about a new privateering commission, asked where he intended to use it. 'Where perhaps the commission might never be seen or heard of,' Tew replied darkly, and offered to buy it for the astounding sum of £500 – which the good Quaker refused.

Undaunted by this rebuff, Tew travelled to New York with his fam-

Tew's pirate flag: the traditional red standard, emblazoned with a white arm clenching a sword.

ily, where they were entertained by the much more pliant Royal Governor, Colonel Benjamin Fletcher. The latter later described Tew as 'what they call a very pleasant man; so that at some times when the labours of my day were over, it was some divertissement as well as information to me, to hear him talk'. But their relationship truly flourished on account of corrupt transactions, which included the purchase of a privateering commission for £300 on 18 November 1694.

Meanwhile Mrs Tew and her two daughters attended gala parties at the Governor's mansion, dressed in rich silks adorned with glittering

diamonds from the Orient, while Fletcher openly bestowed a gold watch upon her husband. Tew also took some pains to write to the *Amity*'s majority owners in Bermuda, alleging that he had not been able to return there as his sloop had sprung a mast, forcing him to pass by although having 'for two weeks beat unsuccessfully against head winds' in a vain attempt to arrive. He further bought their silence by sending them a large payment, reputedly equivalent to fourteen times their original investment in *Amity*.

Once more back at Newport, Tew prepared his sloop for another Far Eastern cruise. When news of this project spread, there was great commotion throughout New England, for word of his deeds had already been carried far and wide. A contemporary chronicler wrote of 'servants from most places of the country running from their masters, sons from their parents', in the hope of signing with Tew. Some lads even tried to get aboard *Amity*, as stowaways. By the end of November 1694 Tew had cleared harbour, and slowly worked his way around the tip of Africa into the Red Sea again.

However, when a second of the Great Moghul's treasure ships was finally encountered in September 1695, the results were drastically different, for in:

... the engagement a shot carried away the rim of Tew's belly, who held his bowels in his hands for some space. When he dropped, it struck such terror to his men that they suffered themselves to be taken without further resistance.

None the less his precedent had already been sufficiently well publicised for many other British privateers to emulate his example, by laying a course for the virgin hunting grounds of the Indian Ocean.

In Jamaica, for example, Governor Sir William Beeston was moved to complain about a dearth of seamen:

> ... for besides the losses through death, the press for the King's ships frightens away many, and many go to the Northern Plantations [*i.e.*, North America], where the Red Sea pirates take their plunder, are pardoned and fit out for a fresh voyage, which makes all kinds of rogues flock to them.

Naturally numerous native New Englanders – such as the Rhode Island tavern-keeper's son William Mayes – also fitted out expeditions of their own, while on the far side of the Atlantic yet another figure was about to follow Tew's inspiration.

Early in 1694, a flotilla of hired British vessels arrived in the Spanish port of La Coruña, in anticipation of departing on a treasure-seeking voyage into the West Indies. Restless at being unpaid after several months, the crew-members mutinied and at 9 o'clock on a Monday night, 7 May 1694, slipped away past the harbour batteries in their 46-gun flagship *Charles II*. The ringleader was a 34-year-old former warrant officer in the Royal Navy named Henry Every, who had been serving as first mate.

Next morning he set his captain and sixteen loyal hands adrift in a boat, saying: 'I am a man of fortune, and must seek my fortune.' Every then convened a meeting of the 85 remaining mutineers who had helped him seize *Charles II*, and persuaded them to embark on a piratical cruise into the Indian Ocean.

His ship was renamed the *Fancy*, and after eighteen months of adventures in the Far East, Every too succeeded in boarding the enormous Moghul trader *Ganj-i-Sawai* off Bombay on 8 September 1695, pillaging it of the staggering sum of £200,000.

He and his men then returned into the Atlantic, and made for the West Indies. By late April 1696 the weather-beaten *Fancy* was dropping anchor at Royal Island off Eleuthera, some fifty miles from New Providence (Nassau) in the Bahamas. Every sent a boat with four men to call upon the corrupt

Henry Every's pirate flag.

local Governor, Nicholas Trott, allegedly identifying himself as 'Henry Bridgeman' and saying his ship was an 'interloper' or unlicensed slaver come from the Guinea Coast of Africa, with a cargo of ivory and slaves. Privately, the Crown official was offered a bribe of £1,000 to allow the raider vessel into port, and its pirates to disperse.

Trott signalled his acquiescence and Every quickly sailed *Fancy* into New Providence, where he and the Governor struck another deal as to the disposal of the craft itself. Still maintaining the fiction that this was a legal transaction, Every made over the ship into the Governor's safe-keeping, 'to take care of her for

use of the owners'. Once this deal was struck, *Fancy* was stripped of everything of value – including 46 guns, one hundred barrels of powder, many small arms, 50 tons of ivory, sails, blocks, etc. – and allowed to drift ashore two days later, to be destroyed by the surf.

With all incriminating evidence thus erased, Every and the majority of his hands disappeared back into civilian life, aboard various passing ships. He was one of the few rovers who fully escaped justice, and like Tew before him, helped provide a new role-model for the whole fraternity of seagoing mercenaries.

Rather than dream of sacking cities at the head of small armies – such as Morgan, Grammont and De Graaf had done a generation earlier – many freebooters now aspired to wealth through a single, solitary capture, with only a handful of followers so as not to debase the shares. The highly spectacular nature of these coups by Tew and Every therefore sapped the buccaneers' military resolve even further.

All this time, while the British had been distracted by these piratical digressions, the war itself had dragged on in the West Indies. By April 1694, the island of Saint-Domingue had recovered sufficient strength for Ducasse to dispatch the *flibustier* Capitaine Beauregard with six of his vessels to prowl the eastern shores of Jamaica. These raiders took a New England ship, but next day HMS *Falcon* sighted the French interlopers and chased them away, recapturing their lone prize.

However, when Beauregard reentered Petit-Goâve a few days later, he found the 50-gun men-of-war *Téméraire* ('Fearless'), *Envieux* ('Envious') and *Solide* ('Wellfound') unexpectedly arrived from France, as escorts for a merchant convoy. This fortuitous occurrence prompted

Left: Eighteenth-century engraving of Henry Every's *Fancy* (centre) capturing the rich Moghul trader *Ganj-i-Sawai* off Bombay, India, on 8 September 1695.

This worthy had departed Jamaica earlier on a smuggling voyage to the Spanish Main, only to be captured by two French corsairs and carried into Saint-Domingue. While being held captive, Elliott had discovered the French plans, stolen a canoe and, with two companions, bravely put to sea during the night of 5 June. Reaching Jamaica five days later, the privateer had stumbled into Governor Beeston's house that evening as he was sitting with some visitors.

Beeston had been astonished at the sight of Elliott, 'in a very mean habit and with a meagre weather-beaten countenance', but more astounded still at his news. The Jamaican Council was immediately convened, and at 9 o'clock that night declared a state of emergency. Work was rushed forward on the harbour fortifications, guns were mounted, troops mustered, ships secured and reinforcements dispatched to outlying areas. By the time the French expedition appeared, the island's defences were fully prepared, although the Jamaicans still remained considerably outnumbered.

Nevertheless these measures proved enough to forestall Ducasse's plan of storming Port Royal, especially as Du Rollon refused to risk any of the King's ships in such a risky undertaking. Consequently the French Governor landed eight hundred men under Beauregard, who marched eastward plundering and destroying all the coastal plantations and homes in his path. From Port Morant boats were also sent around to ravage the northern shores as well, while the British could only look on warily from a safe distance, reluctant to sally for fear of dividing their

Ducasse to contemplate a surprise offensive against Jamaica, first by dispatching the newly arrived squadron into *Falcon*'s patrol area to seize the Royal Naval lookout. This action was accomplished despite the stout resistance offered by the outnumbered *Falcon*, after which the French Governor mustered all his island forces for a devastating assault against his unsuspecting British foes.

Early in June, Ducasse sortied from Petit-Goâve with the *Téméraire* of Capitaine chevalier du Rollon as his flagship, accompanied by *Hasardeux* and *Envieux*. Off Cape Tiburon he gathered a fleet totalling 22 sail and more than 3,000 men (about half of them *flibustiers* under De Graaf), which materialised off the eastern tip of Jamaica on the morning of 27 June 1694, 'in a fresh gale'. Eight of his vessels remained off Port Morant, while the fourteen others anchored in Cow Bay, fifteen miles east of Port Royal. But the French leader then learned that the British had been forewarned, thanks to the heroic efforts of a privateer captain named Stephen Elliott.

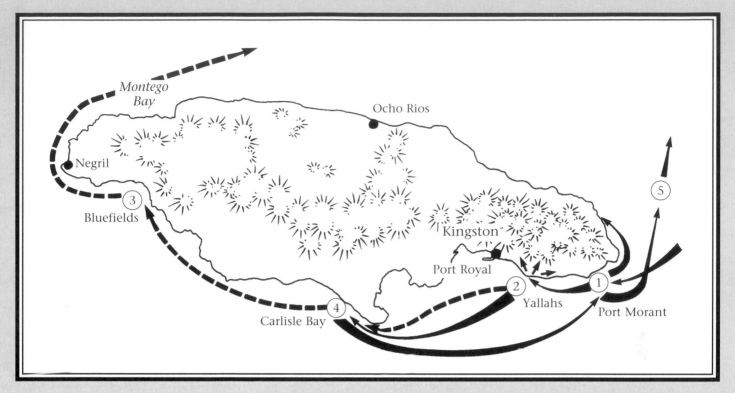

Above: Ducasse and De Graaf's Invasion of Jamaica (Summer 1694): On 27 June 1694, 22 French vessels bearing three thousand men appeared off the eastern tip of Jamaica. Eight anchored off Port Morant (1), the remainder at Yallahs (2), intending to take Port Royal by surprise; but the outnumbered English defenders were so well prepared that Ducasse instead had to ravage the coastal plantations, while his Port Morant contingent visited a like treatment upon the northern shoreline. On July 1st, his 54-gun *Téméraire* and another ship dragged their anchors, being driven downwind (broken line) to Bluefields Bay (3), where the *flibustier* commander Bernanos made a landing before standing away toward Petit-Gôave.

Ducasse meanwhile reunited all his forces at Yallahs, to menace Port Royal by land. When the English sallied, he quickly re-embarked his men and sent all but the three largest ships to assault Carlisle Bay (4) under his deputy, De Graaf. The latter brought 1,400–1,500 *flibustiers* ashore there the night of 28–29 July, easily brushing aside its garrison and pillaging for six days. Rejoined by Ducasse, the French then withdrew on 3 August, retracing their course back to Saint-Domingue (5).

smaller forces with the enemy still to windward of their positions.

On 1 July a sudden gust of wind caused *Téméraire* to drag her anchors, carrying her and another French vessel downwind to Bluefields Bay, where the *flibustier* Jean Bernanos disembarked with 60 men to burn a plantation, before withdrawing. Ducasse meanwhile had been encamped ashore, so continued directing land operations at the eastern end of the island until 27 July, when he mustered the bulk of his forces in Cow Bay and began threatening Port Royal.

When Beeston sortied to contest this latest French manoeuvre, Ducasse quickly re-embarked his men under cover of darkness and sent all but the three largest ships scurrying 35 miles downwind, to assault Carlisle Bay under his second in command, De Graaf. This contingent dropped anchor opposite that town in the afternoon of the 28th, landing 1,400–1,500 *flibustiers* that night. Next morning they assailed the 250-man local garrison, Beauregard commanding the van, while De Graaf brought up the main body.

After driving out the British militia, foraging parties were sent out to scour the surrounding countryside, but with only limited success as each plantation constituted a miniature fortress, impossible to breach without artillery. As the French did not have time to bring any siege guns ashore, they satisfied themselves with carrying off whatever they could, which booty was hastily transferred aboard once Ducasse rejoined a few days later. The French chieftain then weighed and returned to Port Morant, before quitting Jamaica altogether on 3 August, and re-entering Petit-Goâve on the 14th.

Despite having spent a month and a half wreaking total havoc throughout this prostrate British colony, his huge throng of *flibustiers* were disappointed at their spoils. They had brought off 1,600 slaves and a seemingly impressive amount of plunder, but this dwindled once it had to be redistributed among so many. Hence the notion that large campaigns did not pay was further underscored, while it soon became evident these could provoke heavy

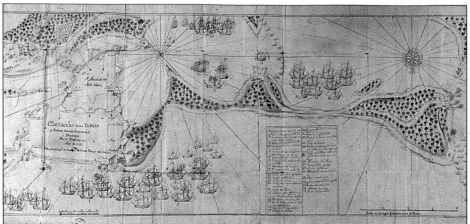

Left: French fleets drawn up before Cartagena, as seen by a Spanish eye-witness. (Archivo General de Indias, Seville, Spain)

retaliation as well. Late that following month Beeston sent a small force of three British men-of-war, a fireship and two barques to exact some measure of vengeance. These bombarded the village of l'Esterre near Léogâne on 11 October 1694, then bore down menacingly upon Petit-Goâve, only to sheer off when they realised Beauregard had rallied the local *boucaniers* and *habitants* to resist them. A few huts were burnt on Île-à-Vache, before the Jamaicans disappeared over the horizon.

Not for long, though, as next spring an expedition arrived in the Antilles from England, consisting of two dozen vessels and almost one thousand troops under Colonel Luke Lillingston and Commodore Robert Wilmot. These joined forces with another sizeable contingent of Spaniards out of Santo Domingo and three men-of-war from the Armada de Barlovento, which together fell upon Cap-François on 15 May 1695. Now it was the Frenchmen's turn to suffer, as this huge force brushed aside the heavily outnumbered defenders under De Graaf – even capturing his wife and two children – before sweeping destructively along that island's north-western shoreline.

One month later the Royal Naval squadron had reached as far as Port-de-Paix, where it deposited five hundred British troops who skirmished with its garrison, until the main Spanish army could arrive overland. The French then became besieged within their town, surrounded by terrified loved ones, until eventually they decided to evacuate two hours before dawn on 15 July, only to be caught in an ambush and massacred. Among the dead was 47-year-old Capitaine Bernanos, a great *flibustier* who was to be remembered as 'the bravest man there ever was in the colony', but whose courage and skill were futile against such a vast enemy host. The British and Spanish allies then sailed away on the 27th, having levelled Port-de-Paix.

No major campaigns could be mounted the following year, as all belligerents were becoming drained by the war, although Ducasse did receive word that a counter-expedition would soon be sent out from France under Bernard-Jean-Louis de Saint-Jean, baron de Pointis, for which he should raise a large contingent of *flibustier* auxiliaries. This fleet did not actually depart Brest until 7 January 1697, however, by which time the first peace overtures were already being exchanged in Europe. Because of the bankruptcy of the French exchequer, Louis XIV furnished only the ships, crews and men, while wealthy private citizens raised the necessary financing for wages, supplies and provisions, in expectation of a handsome return. Their intent was to make a lucrative assault on the great Spanish-American port of Cartagena before hostilities ceased.

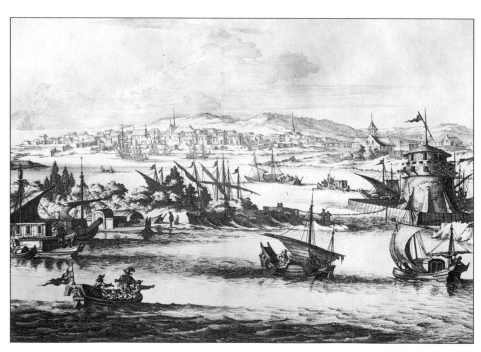

Left: Cartagena, Colombia, as depicted by a seventeenth-century Dutch artist.

Pointis's ten ships-of-the-line, four frigates and several troop transports appeared off Cap-François in early March 1697, with 2,800 soldiers aboard, and by the 16th his 84-gun flagship *Sceptre* was dropping anchor before Petit-Goâve. But when Ducasse came aboard, the French admiral was infuriated to learn that only a few hundred buccaneers had awaited him, the rest having dispersed on their own pursuits because of his late arrival. Relations worsened a day later when a French naval officer arrested an unruly *boucanier* ashore, touching off a riot in which two or three others died. Only the personal intervention of Ducasse succeeded in calming the mob.

The freebooters, for their part, resented the secondary role they were being offered in this enterprise, with the question of shares being kept deliberately vague and Ducasse excluded from any command position. None the less they enlisted in fair numbers once Pointis proclaimed that they would all participate 'man for man' with the crews of his royal warships, and Ducasse offered to go as a ship's captain aboard his 40-gun *Pontchartrain*, directing the island contingent.

In this manner a force of 170 Saint-Domingue soldiers, 110 volunteers, 180 free blacks and 650 *flibustiers* was raised, sailing aboard *Serpente*, 18; *Gracieuse* ('Graceful'), 20; *Cerf Volant* ('Kite'), 18; *Saint Louis*, 18; *Dorade* ('Golden One'), 16; *Marie, Françoise* and one other vessel, all of which rendezvoused off Cape Tiburon with the main fleet and by 8 April 1697 were in sight of the Spanish Main. Five days later they dropped anchor before the city of Cartagena proper.

Pointis's strategy was a crude one: he proposed to disembark the buccaneers immediately on the outskirts of the startled city, supported by his warships' covering fire. But once Ducasse and Pointis actually reconnoitred the shoreline in a boat, they found it lined with dangerous reefs (their own craft capsizing, so that they barely escaped drowning). It was therefore decided to force the harbour entrance further to the south, at Bocachica, and on the 15th

Ducasse and Pointis disembarked at the nearby hamlet of Los Hornos with 1,200 men.

While preparing their siege operations against Bocachica's fortress, the buccaneers captured a coaster arriving from Portobelo and also drove off some Spanish reinforcements who were stealing down from Cartagena in boats. During this latter skirmish some freebooters came under fire from the fort itself, which caused them to scatter. Mistaking this for military indiscipline, Pointis fell upon them with a cudgel and henceforth began treating

Opposite page: Map published by Admiral de Pointis, showing the city and harbour of Cartagena

the *flibustiers* with ever increasing contempt. Bocachica surrendered after a token assault on the 16th, during which six French soldiers and seven buccaneers were killed and 22 wounded, among the latter Ducasse.

His *flibustier* contingent therefore came under the orders of his second in command, Joseph d'Honon de Gallifet, a relative newcomer to Saint-Domingue who was not well known to the rank-and-file. Meanwhile the French continued to advance by both land and sea against Cartagena, first coming up with Fort Santa Cruz, which they found abandoned. At this point Pointis ordered the buccaneers to detach and circle round the Spanish positions to seize the Nuestra Señora de la Popa high ground behind the city, while his main army continued its direct approach overland.

There was considerable hesitation among the *flibustiers* at this command, until Honon de Gallifet seized a buccaneer by the arm to force him toward the boats, at which he was thrown off. Pointis immediately intervened by having the offender tied to a tree and blindfolded, in anticipation of being executed by regular musketeers. But in a contrived gesture, Honon publicly interceded and Pointis agreed to release this man, so as to ingratiate the new *flibustier* commander with his followers. The buccaneers eventually departed somewhat grudgingly on their mission, but were relieved to find the Spaniards had fled before them, and so their thrust was able to occupy the heights

Right: Pointis and Ducasse's Assault on Cartagena (April 1697): During an initial bombardment of this city (1), the French failed to find a quick disembarkation point (2), so moved further south to attempt its Bocachica entrance. A force of 1,200 *flibustiers* and regular troops were landed at Los Hornos (3), while warships menaced Fort San Luis (4). Having taken this place, the French then advanced by both land and water against Fort Santa Cruz (5), which they found abandoned. The *flibustier* contingent next rounded to Los Tejares (6) to gain the Popa high ground (7), while the main body drove directly towards Cartagena. Finding Fort San Lázaro empty, the two prongs reunited and began siege operations against the Getsemaní suburb (8). Having breached this perimeter, they reached the inner walls and forced the Spaniards to surrender on 4 May.

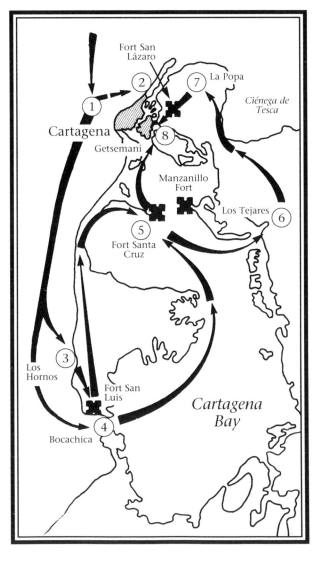

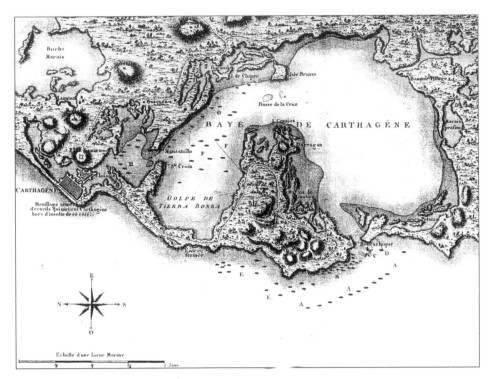

unopposed and link up with the main army by the 20th.

A formal siege of Cartagena's suburb of Getsemaní ensued, with approach trenches being dug and heavy artillery landed from the French fleet. During these operations Pointis sustained a leg wound from a Spanish sharpshooter, so continued supervising the works from a litter. On 28 April a heavy bombardment began, and during a lull in this firing on the 30th, Ducasse – now recuperated from his injury – visited a Spanish officer at the gate and noticed a fair breach had been made in one wall.

At his urging, Pointis ordered an immediate assault for 4 o'clock that afternoon, and in bloody hand-to-hand combat French grenadiers and *flibustiers* fought their way through this gap to the very edge of Cartagena itself. The defenders' morale collapsed, and on the evening of 2 May white flags were hoisted over their walls. While settling the terms of surrender, Pointis received word that a Spanish relief column of more than one thousand men was approaching, so promptly sent Ducasse and his buccaneers to

oppose them, together with several hundred regular soldiers.

This Spanish force never appeared, and in the meantime Pointis occupied Cartagena on 4 May. By the time Ducasse and his men returned to that city, they found the gates closed and they were billeted in the impoverished, devastated Getsemaní suburb. The French commander-in-chief evidently feared that they would violate his carefully arranged capitulation terms, so kept them outside its walls, and away from where the booty was being tallied. The few remaining Spanish inhabitants were obliged to surrender most of their wealth as tribute, and the total plunder eventually came to eight million French crowns.

The impatient buccaneers expected to receive a quarter of this as their share, but were outraged when at the end of the month they discovered they were only assigned forty thousand crowns. Unbeknown to them, the naval crews aboard Pointis's warships had been serving for only a small percentage of the whole, which is what he had meant when he deceitfully offered

them equal shares 'man for man'. By now the bulk of this plunder was already aboard his men-of-war, ready to depart.

Furious at being duped, the *flibustiers* swarmed back into Cartagena on 30 May – despite Ducasse's attempts to dissuade them – and rounded-up every Spaniard they could find, herding these into the principal church and sprinkling them with gunpowder, which they threatened to ignite unless an additional five million crowns were produced forthwith. This was clearly impossible, but through brutal tortures and extortion the buccaneers succeeded in raising a thousand crowns per man, before weighing on 3 June.

In the interim Pointis had also departed, but four days later had encountered the large fleet of the British Vice-Admiral John Neville and his Dutch allies at sea, hastening to Cartagena's rescue. Outnumbered and with most of his crews dead or diseased, Pointis instantly reversed course and evaded his pursuers over the next two days, until he finally shook them off at sun-up on 10 June. This chase had carried Neville very near to Cartagena, which he visited briefly before roaming north-eastward, and on the 25th sighted Ducasse at anchor with his eight laggard buccaneer vessels off Sambay.

In addition to having been cheated by Pointis, the *flibustiers* now found themselves involved in a close pursuit by a fleet of hostile men-of-war. During this chase the British quickly overtook *Gracieuse* and the 50-gun '*Christe*' (possibly a Spanish prize originally named *Santo Cristo*), as well as driving Capitaine Charles's *Saint Louis* hard aground. He and his crew managed to escape ashore, only to be hunted down and captured by the local Spaniards, who put them to work as convict labourers in rebuilding Cartagena's shattered defences. Neville then detached four of his

men o' war to continue shadowing Ducasse's remaining vessels, which scattered in the general direction of Saint-Domingue. Capitaine Macary's *Cerf Volant* was driven on to the rocks off that coast, but the rest straggled into their home ports safely.

None the less, *flibustier* morale had been dealt a near fatal blow, from which it would never fully recover. Large land operations fell completely out of vogue, except for certain isolated incidents. Henceforth rovers of every stripe began to lapse into their old piratical ways, with small bands eking out a living as commerce raiders or naval auxiliaries during wartime, or seagoing brigands during peacetime. Gone were the heady days when mighty multi-national coalitions might form off some uninhabited tropical isle, to seize any Spanish–American city they chose. Such combinations were now seen as profitless, and their commanders shunned as international pariahs by European colonial officials, rather than courted as the coveted mercenary leaders they had once been.

Even the 'Pirate Round' faded from existence, as civilian authorities imposed stricter measures against returning rovers, while furthermore the natives of Madagascar rose in revolt against Baldridge and his men in 1697, forcing them to flee Saint Mary's because of the number of local blacks they had sold into bondage. Thus this former 'King of the Pirates' travelled to New York, where he settled down and lived to a ripe old age. Ironically, his expulsion occurred just as one of the last major seventeenth-century forays entered the Pacific, led by yet another New Yorker, ostensibly intended as a sweep against pirates.

Two years earlier, Captain William Kidd had sailed to London in hopes of obtaining a privateering commission. These were not readily available, so he entered into a scheme with the influential Earl of Bellomont, whereby such a licence might be granted. This nobleman was in need of money, and about to be appointed Governor of New England: consequently he agreed to gather investors and secure a patent from his friends in the Whig government, which would allow Kidd to outfit a ship and hunt pirates in the Far East. Since the latter were making a rich haul, Kidd would be able to impound their booty and carry it to New England for adjudication, where the Earl and other investors need pay no royal duties, and so reap a handsome profit.

A privateering commission was duly issued to Kidd on 26 January 1696 (Old Style), allowing him to seek out rovers such as Thomas Tew and William Mayes, a most unusual concession for any vessel except a Royal Naval warship. The brand-new frigate-galley *Adventure*, of 34 guns, 287 tons and 46 sweeps, was also bought at Deptford, and seventy hard-bitten seamen recruited on the basis of 'no purchase, no pay'. *Adventure* quit London in April 1696, traversing the Atlantic to New York, where Kidd announced a cruise to the Red Sea, and quickly had 152 men on board (some coming from as far away as Philadelphia). On 6 September 1696 (Old Style) he bid farewell to his wife and daughters and got under way.

Rounding the Cape of Good Hope, *Adventure* fell in with the Royal Naval squadron of Commodore Thomas Warren that December. Sailing in company for a week, Kidd feared that Warren would impress many of his seamen, so when the ships became becalmed, he rowed out of sight. Warren entered the Cape Colony convinced that Kidd intended to turn pirate, which was confirmed when *Adventure* attacked the peaceful Mocha trading fleet in August 1697, only to be driven off by the 36-gun British East Indiaman *Sceptre*. Other attacks soon followed, until at last, towards the end of January 1698, Kidd finally succeeded in capturing a rich prize, the 400-ton *Quedah Merchant* out of Surat, India, which carried a French pass and £30,000 in cargo. It took him a few weeks to dispose of some of its goods, then several months before he touched at the abandoned pirate lair of Madagascar to beach and

Left: Soldier firing an arquebus

daughters met him off Oyster Pond Bay a few days later, and Kidd discovered the full extent of his infamy: honest merchants regarded him as a villainous pirate, while rougher spirits believed he was returning with untold wealth, so that he worriedly sent a secret message to his patron Bellomont – who had been installed as New England's Governor little more than a year before – to find out where he stood.

Bellomont returned a letter from Boston assuring Kidd of protection, but hinting at certain unforeseen complications. *San Antonio* reluctantly put into port, where Kidd met the Governor on the weekend of 1/2 July 1699 (Old Style), before presenting himself before the Massachusetts Council that Monday. Although everything seemed to go well at first, Kidd was arrested when he returned to testify on Thursday the 6th, despite rushing into the chamber and crying out for Bellomont's assistance as the constables closed in. The Governor did not intervene as Kidd was dragged away and gaoled, nor when he was deported to England the following spring to stand trial and be executed. The world of the pirate was indeed changing, when such a welcome awaited any Red Sea-man returning home heavily laden with booty.

burn *Adventure* before heading home in his prize.

Early in April 1699 *Quedah Merchant* made her landfall off Anguilla Island in the West Indies, where Kidd took on fresh provisions. Here he learned that the East India Company factors in India had been arrested by the Moghul in retaliation for his depredation, so that 'John Company' had now declared him a pirate and instituted a global man-hunt. He therefore sought asylum at Danish Saint Thomas but was rejected, so hovered uneasily off Mona Island between Puerto Rico and Santo Domingo, selling off his Indian wares while attempting to buy another ship.

He eventually purchased the sloop *San Antonio* and crept stealthily back into lower Delaware Bay at the beginning of June, hoping to avoid detection. His wife and

Typical West Indian brigantine.

128

VIII

Pirate Swan-Song

Dying is a pleasure,
When living is a pain.
John Dryden (1631–1700)

The very year after Kidd was executed in 1701, the peace following the Nine Years War was shattered by the eruption of the War of the Spanish Succession in Europe (becoming known as Queen Anne's War in America). The reason for this renewed round of hostilities was that the last Habsburg king of Spain, the pathetic 39-year-old imbecile Charles II, had died without issue, leaving the French Bourbon princeling Philip of Anjou as his closest male heir. The other major European powers objected to this union of French and Spanish interests, fearing that it would result in a single all-powerful overseas empire under Philip's grandfather, Louis XIV. Consequently, a 'Grand Alliance' was formed between Britain, Holland, Prussia, Austria, Hanover and Portugal, to oppose this transfer by force of arms, British passions being further aroused by Louis' continual efforts to restore the exiled Catholic Stuart monarch, James II, to their throne.

For West Indian privateers, this new war marked yet another significant shift in their alignments, the French *flibustiers* now finding themselves reluctant allies of their former enemies – and favourite victims – the Spanish–Americans. The previous Nine Years conflict had already broken the long association

between Jamaican privateers and Saint-Domingue's *flibustiers*, which in the past had produced such formidable military combinations, as well as a steady peacetime employment for both. This latest change meant that France's Caribbean corsairs could no longer raid the Main, nor attack any Spanish shipping; instead, French warships were being assigned to protect Spanish convoys.

It is one of the small ironies of pirate history that Ducasse, the former Governor of Saint-Domingue and leader of its *flibustiers*, was among the very first officers relegated to such a duty. A few years after his expedition against Cartagena with Pointis, Ducasse retired from the governorship and returned to France. But immediately upon the outbreak of this latest war, he was promoted commodore (*chef*

Right: Spanish galleon.

129

d'escadre) in France's royal navy, and dispatched to Madrid to secure the Spanish–American slave *asiento* for French commercial interests. Once there he had further been appointed admiral or *capitán general* in Spain's royal navy by the French-born Philip V, then sent to escort a silver convoy across the Atlantic to the New World.

Ducasse left Cadiz in his flagship *Heureux* ('Happy') with three other French ships of the line, plus a frigate, re-entering Cartagena only five years after he had helped lay it waste, this time as a most unexpected ally. He soon proved his worth by winning the first major encounter of the war: while escorting a troop transport past Santa Marta on 29 August 1702, he became involved in a five-day running fight against a superior British force of seven ships of the line under Admiral John Benbow. Despite being outnumbered, Ducasse succeeded in repelling the numerous British assaults, during which his opponent was abandoned by most of his commanders and eventually mortally wounded. (This action became known in Royal Naval history as 'Admiral Benbow's Last Fight'; four of his captains were later court-martialled for cowardice, two of them receiving the death penalty.)

But such set-piece fleet engagements were to remain very much the exception during the forthcoming eleven years of conflict, as the War of the Spanish Succession quickly devolved into a global contest of commercial interceptions and blockades. This strategy contributed to the final erosion of the privateers' military skill, as they naturally preferred hunting alone for easy prizes at sea, and so lost the last of their martial aspirations. One of the few large land raids came late in the war when the legendary French corsair René Duguay-Trouin attacked the Portuguese colony of Rio de Janeiro. Like Pointis's expedi-

Pirate prey: forsaking military aspirations, West Indian privateers increasingly began turning their efforts against softer targets during the early eighteenth century, such as these rich merchant travellers.

tion, Duguay-Trouin's ships and men were furnished by the Crown, but his financing was raised by private subscription, and the affair was intended more for securing booty than any territorial gain. He set sail with fifteen men-of-war (seven of them ships of the line) and two thousand troops, boldly forcing the entrance to this South American port and capturing it on 21 September 1711. Five Portuguese men-of-war and 60 merchantmen were either seized or destroyed, after which the raiders received a hefty ransom to withdraw.

Thus by the time peace was finally declared in the spring of 1713, a new generation of privateers had emerged that had never fought a significant action on land. Their inclination was entirely towards commercial raiding, and a majority were British, this power having emerged triumphant from the naval contest. (Both France and Britain lost about 1,500 merchant vessels apiece during the war, but while the former's overseas trade had been ruined as a result, the British had weathered this storm much better, emerging more powerful at sea and with an expanded colonial empire. Even more ominous for seafaring renegades, the Royal Navy was also becoming increasingly professional, beginning operations on a permanent year-round basis and making the Caribbean less safe than before for rogue elements.)

Saint-Domingue was now out of bounds because of France's new relationship with Spain, so those marauders who refused to renounce fighting once peace was promulgated, sought refuge amid the Bahamas. They found these strategically placed islands temporarily uninhabited, because they had been so repeatedly sacked and burned by the Spanish and French during the previous hostilities, that the few English settlers had abandoned them in despair. Into this void came the privateers, who discovered the port of New Providence (Nassau) especially well suited to their purposes: its harbour was too shallow and tricky for heavy men-of-war to enter easily, while the surrounding hills afforded excellent vantage points for espying passing ships. Furthermore, the island's reefs teemed with lobster, fish and turtle, and the well-wooded interior featured fresh-water springs and an abundance of fruit and game.

Within a few years, several hundred of the most notorious West Indian buccaneers were operating out of this archipelago. In short order they began making a nuisance of themselves under commanders such as Thomas Barrow, Charles Vane and Benjamin Hornigold, by waylaying peaceful merchantmen travelling to and from the Caribbean. 'A nest of pirates are endeavouring to establish themselves in New Providence,' Governor Alexander Spotswood of

Right: Spanish settlement in Florida.

Virginia reported to London in July 1716, adding that they seemed bound to convert it into 'a second Madagascar'. Soon these pirates grew ever more brazen, raiding the eastern seaboard of North America as far as Maine. 'I am a free prince,' one such marauder – Charles Bellamy – roared at the captain of a Boston merchant ship he captured off South Carolina in 1717, 'and I have as much authority to make war on the whole world as he who has a hundred sail of ships at sea, and an army of one hundred thousand men in the field.' But such boastful declarations masked a hidden fear, as Bellamy himself probably realised, because of the rovers' palpable decline as a force.

Even so, Royal Naval patrols out of the West Indies could not dig these elusive pirates out of their lair, but only provide naval escorts for convoys until they were past the Bahamas. A consortium of private London merchants therefore decided to act, banding together to form a syndicate which leased the Bahamas from the Crown, with the intent of resettling them with a more honest citizenry. To head this enterprise, they chose one of the most experienced adventurers of that day: a Dorset sea captain in his late thirties named Woodes Rogers, who had circumnavigated the globe during the previous war in command of two privateer vessels, and captured the Manila galleon off the coast of California. Himself a firm believer in establishing colonies in every corner of the world to promote Britain's trade, Rogers was eager for this latest challenge. The Crown further underwrote his efforts by promising one hundred foot soldiers towards a

Right: Charles Vane, the renegade who impudently defied the new Governor-elect of the Bahamas, Woodes Rogers.

Right: John Rackham, known as 'Calico Jack' for his penchant of wearing bright cotton clothing, was chosen by Vane's crew as their new captain. He is best remembered as the lover of Anne Bonney.

new garrison, plus an escort of warships.

In the autumn of 1717, George I appointed Rogers 'Captain-General and Governor-in-Chief in and over our Bahama Islands in America', and authorised him to wipe out its pirates in any way he chose, including the granting of royal pardons. Final preparations were made that winter, with stores, materials and tools being gathered for the 250 new colonists (plus tracts from the Society for Promoting Christian Knowledge, in the hope of weaning cut-throat pirates from their wicked ways). Finally, on 11 April 1718 (O.S.), Rogers stood down the Thames aboard his flagship, the 460-ton East Indiaman *Delicia*, and was joined off the coast by the frigates HMSS *Milford* and *Rose*. These, with the naval sloops *Buck* and *Shark*, struck out together into the Atlantic.

Three months later Rogers' expedition came within sight of the Bahamas, dropping anchor outside the bar of New Providence proper on the afternoon of 24 July (Old Style). Word of his mission had already preceded him, and soon some of the original English inhabitants rowed out from nearby Harbour Island to greet their new Governor. They informed him that about one thousand pirates remained inside the roadstead, a majority being willing to forswear their illegal activities in exchange for a King's pardon. The more recalcitrant had already decamped for other bases, except Charles Vane, whose anchored flagship would have to be dealt with.

That night, Rogers sent *Rose* and *Shark* probing into the harbour, with local pilots on board, to take soundings. Vane saw them approach and set ablaze a recently captured French prize which he had fitted out as a fire-ship. This drifted menacingly towards *Rose* out of the darkness, bursting into a wild display of flames and loud explosions which sent the Royal Naval frigate and sloop scurrying back out to sea, although undamaged. The following dawn Vane ran up the flag of Saint George to his maintopmast head, and his own personal black pirate flag to the mizzen, before firing a single derisory salute and getting under way. Thoroughly familiar with this harbour, he began threading his way through its eastern narrows towards the open sea, while Rogers unsuccessfully tried to cut off his escape.

(Vane later sent back word that he would return and burn *Delicia* in revenge for this pursuit, although like many other pirate utterances, this proved to be mere braggadocio. In fact Vane was voted out of his captaincy a few months later, for failing to engage a French ship. He was succeeded in command by John 'Calico Jack' Rackham, who turned Vane and his few adherents adrift in a small sloop. Vane soon recouped his fortunes, seizing numerous larger vessels until he was shipwrecked in the Bay of Honduras. After a lengthy period marooned on a tiny island, he was rescued, only to be recognised by an old acquaintance and carried into Jamaica, where he was hanged.)

When Rogers finally stepped ashore at New Providence on the morning of 27 July (Old Style), he was greeted by an honour guard of three hundred unkempt, boozy pirates drawn up into two long lines. At the shouted commands of their captains – Hornigold, Thomas Burgess and others – these fired ragged volleys over the new Governor's head, accompanied by long huzzas for George I. Rogers progressed solemnly to the edge of the town's single small fort, from whose crumbling ramparts he read aloud the commission appointing him Governor of the Bahamas, plus the royal proclamation pardoning pirates. No hint of opposition was raised to this investiture, and the fierce rovers meekly sought out their pardons. Eventually more than six hundred were issued, as Rogers brought his troops and settlers ashore, and offered the marauders a free plot of land for any who chose to clear it and build a house within a year, which some did.

The new Governor also commissioned Hornigold and Burgess as privateer commanders for the islands, and organised New Providence's buccaneers into three militia companies, for a better defence. Unfortunately he soon found their military qualities sadly deteriorated, so that when a renewed war between Britain and Spain threatened that autumn, the ex-pirates proved highly inept militiamen. 'These wretches can't be kept to watch at night,' Rogers noted with exasperation, adding that 'when they do come [on duty, they are]

very seldom sober, and rarely awake all night, though our officers or soldiers very often surprise their guard and carry off their arms, and I punish, fine or confine them almost every day.'

Indeed, those renegades who possessed the greatest pugnacity were seemingly the ones who had quit the Bahamas prior to Rogers' arrival. Chief among these was the hulking brute born Edward Teach or Thatch, but forever immortalised as 'Black-

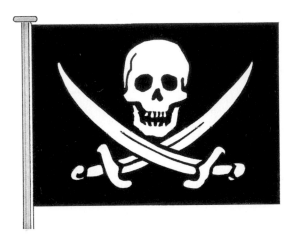

Above: Rackham's pirate flag.

beard'. He had learned his trade as a privateersman during the war, then served a turn under Hornigold. By late 1716 Blackbeard had his own ship, *Queen Anne's Revenge*, a 40-gun French vessel captured off the Antillean island of Saint Vincent. His imposing size, wrathful temperament and lunatic antics made him a force among the buccaneers, while his primitive skills were sufficiently well-honed to beat off an attack by the 30-gun frigate HMS *Scarborough* the following year, as well as obliging four vessels to surrender to him without a fight in the Bay of Honduras.

But when word began spreading of Rogers' impending arrival at New Providence to restore government rule, Blackbeard was among those who chose to sail away to the Carolinas, rather than remain. He and his consorts arrived off that coast

and in January 1718 obtained a pardon from North Carolina's Governor Charles Eden and his Council, under the Act of Grace. These officials were willing to overlook the pirates' chequered past for a share of their loot, as their colony was quite poor and without any appreciable trade. Soon Blackbeard and his followers began basing themselves around Cape Fear, and once more took up their old practice of waylaying passing merchantmen and selling the plunder at cut-rate prices up the Pamlico River, in the town of Bath.

By spring, the renegades had grown so bold as to blockade Charleston, the capital of the neighbouring colony of South Carolina. Within the space of one week, Blackbeard seized eight or nine ships sailing in or out of its harbour, as well as holding hostage Samuel Wragg, a member of that colony's Council, together with his 4-year-old son. The pirate chieftain even threatened to kill both and send their heads to Governor Robert Johnson, as well as 'burn the ships that lay before the town and beat it about our ears', if the South Carolinians did not provide him and his pirates with urgently needed medical supplies. The Governor eventually complied by sending out a chest containing £300–£400 worth of medicines – most probably mercurial drugs for the treatment of syphilis – but such rash, extortionate methods were not easily forgotten, nor forgiven.

By June 1718, Blackbeard's flotilla had swollen to four ships, several small tenders and perhaps a total of four hundred men, but these numbers were somewhat misleading. His minions were a far cry from the disciplined mercenaries who had dominated the Caribbean during that previous century, nor could the uncouth Blackbeard and his captains be compared to the great commanders of the past, men such as Morgan, De Graaf or Grammont. For in addition to his own intemperate, self–destructive impulses, Blackbeard's lieutenants included individuals such as Major Stede Bonnet, one of the most peculiar of all pirates.

Bonnet had been born a gentleman, was well educated, and had served honourably in the war before retiring from the army to his estate on the West Indian island of Barbados. Why he should choose to go on a peacetime privateering cruise remains a mystery, his acquaintances later attributing it to 'a disorder of his mind'. None the less, he purchased a 10-gun sloop, hired a crew of 70 men and set out on his new career. Bonnet bumbled ineffectually about the Caribbean until he encountered Blackbeard, who laughed openly at this amateurish gentleman pirate and impressed his sloop into his flotilla.

Bonnet remained under Blackbeard's orders for several months before finally separating from him in the summer of 1718, to go off on his own account. This independent cruise proved short-lived, for a few weeks later Bonnet was captured with 30 of his men in the Cape Fear river, after a battle with two sloops sent out by the vengeful Governor of South Carolina. Carried into Charleston, Bonnet escaped, only to be recaptured, tried and executed in November 1718. It was said that many people were moved by his 'piteous behaviour under sentence', but there was now no mercy for pirates. Bonnet died ignominiously at the end of a rope, being turned off from the cart's tail on the Charleston waterfront only a few days before the fearsome Blackbeard himself also met his end.

That pirate chieftain had seen his flotilla dwindle and disperse, being reduced to little more than a score of followers aboard his one remaining sloop, the *Adventure*. But Blackbeard refused to abandon his station off Cape Fear, and in the autumn of 1718 Governor Spotswood of Virginia received word that the pirate had carried a captured merchantman into North Carolina's Ocracoke Inlet, which he intended to turn into a fortified

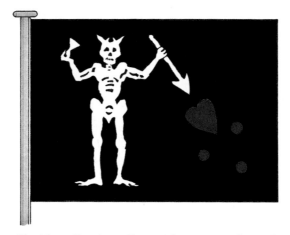

Blackbeard's pirate flag, with a crowned Death-figure clutching an hourglass in one hand, indicating his opponent's time was running out, while the other stabs at a pierced heart.

base. The Governor detested pirates in general and Blackbeard in particular, having already persuaded the Virginia Assembly to post a £100 reward for his capture (and £40 for other pirate captains, £20 for lieutenants, masters, quartermasters, boatswains and carpenters, and £10 for ordinary seamen). Notwithstanding the fact that Blackbeard's vessel was clearly in North Carolina's jurisdiction, Spotswood decided to act by sending an agent to survey this situation, and bring back a pair of coastal pilots familiar with its local inshore inlets.

The Governor then prepared an expedition in utmost secrecy, 'for fear of Blackbeard's having intelligence, there being in this country an unaccountable inclination to

favour pirates'. Virginia had two Royal Naval men-of-war as guard ships in the James river, HMSS *Pearl* and *Lyme*, but these drew too much water to penetrate Ocracoke Inlet. Spotswood therefore hired two shallow-draught sloops and manned one of these with 35 men under Lieutenant Robert Maynard of HMS *Pearl*, and the other with 25 men under Midshipman Baker of HMS *Lyme*. Both got under way from Chesapeake Bay at 3 o'clock on the afternoon of 17 November 1718 (Old Style), and late on the afternoon of the 21st came within sight of Ocracoke Inlet. After spotting their quarry inside, Maynard and Baker stood into its entrance and dropped anchor to await the dawn.

An unconcerned Blackbeard spent that night carousing with his nineteen men, and at first light it was the Royal Naval pair that moved first. Manoeuvring across the inlet with some difficulty in the gloom, they drew near the *Adventure* until Blackbeard himself at last hailed: 'Damn you for villains, who are you?'

Maynard responded by running up the British ensign and shouting back: 'You may see by our colours we are no pirates.'

Blackbeard roared out that they should come aboard so that he could personally see who they were, to which Maynard replied: 'I cannot spare my boat, but I will come aboard of you as soon as I can, with my sloop!'

This implicit threat to carry the pirate sloop by storm sent Blackbeard into a rage, during which he spluttered: 'Damnation seize my soul if I give you quarters, or take any from you!'

Maynard hollered back in a similar vein, at which Blackbeard ran up his black ensign with its death's-head insignia, cut his cables, and began sliding *Adventure* down chan-

Above: Contemporary portrait of the bug-eyed Edward Teach, 'commonly call'd Black Beard', festooned with firearms and with slow-matches smouldering in his hair, to frighten his victims.

Above: Portly, clean-shaven and bewigged, Major Stede Bonnet was such an unlikely pirate that Blackbeard burst into gales of laughter when the two met off the South Carolina coast in 1718.

nel towards the open sea. Baker tried to block this escape with his sloop, at which the pirate veered and loosed off a vicious broadside, killing Baker and several of his crew, and setting the Royal Naval sloop helplessly adrift. But the faint morning breeze then died away, so that in frustration Maynard ordered his own crew to man their sweeps, and closed upon *Adventure* with his one remaining vessel. When he came within range, the pirates opened up a withering fire upon Maynard's sloop, wounding many of his crew and forcing the Royal Naval officer to order most of his men below, out of the line of fire. Only he, a midshipman and a North Carolina pilot remained above decks, exposed to the rovers' fire.

Sensing his opponent's weakness, Blackbeard worked *Adventure* up against Maynard's sloop, and showered it with glass hand-grenades (bottles filled with powder, small shot and scrap iron, garlanded with lighted fuses). When the smoke from these blasts cleared, Blackbeard noticed that the Royal Naval vessel's decks were almost entirely empty, and shouted at his men that their enemies were 'all knock'd on the head, except three or four; and therefore let's jump aboard, and cut

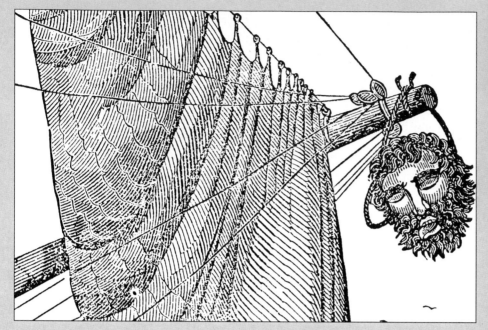

Left: Blackbeard's head being conveyed back to Virginia on Maynard's bowsprit.

Left: Despite desperate pleas for mercy, Bonnet was turned off from the cart's tail at the waterfront of Charleston, South Carolina, in November of 1718, clutching a nosegay.

them to pieces'. He himself was the first to vault across, and lash the sloops together with rope.

But at that moment Maynard shouted down his hatches and ordered all remaining men on deck, much to the pirates' dismay. Nonplussed, the huge Blackbeard waded furiously into the Navy men's midst, hacking and slashing until he came face-to-face with Maynard, who shot him with a pistol. Howling mad, the pirate immediately swung his cutlass and snapped the officer's blade in half, but before he could finish Maynard off, a seaman slashed Blackbeard across the throat with a sword. Surrounded by a pack of sailors, the ogre was then repeatedly shot, hacked and stabbed until he toppled over dead, at which his followers surrendered. Ten pirates had been killed in this vicious mêlée, the remaining nine wounded, as opposed to ten of Maynard's men dead and 24 wounded. The Royal Naval officer then concluded the day by ordering Blackbeard's body to be decapitated, so that the head could be brought back to Virginia dangling from his sloop's bowsprit.

The death of Blackbeard (and of several other lesser pirate captains at about this same time), plus the earlier re-occupation of New Providence, signalled to the remaining renegades that the Americas were now becoming distinctly too warm for them. Choosing the path of least resistance, they sought easier pickings by crossing the Atlantic to Africa and the Far East, perhaps hopeful of reviving the ancient 'Pirate Round' – although unlike

Condent's pirate banner.

their precursors from the 1690s, this generation was noticeably not motivated by a lack of potential prizes in the New World, but rather by an excess of official retaliation.

Among the first to renew operations off Africa was Edward England, while his collegue Christopher Condent visited the former pirate haunt of Madagascar before venturing northward into the Arabian Sea. Near Bombay the latter had the great good fortune to take an Arab ship with a cargo of approximately £150,000 in gold and silver, which yielded shares of nigh on £2,000 for each of his men. When his company broke up after this fabulous share-out at Saint Mary's in Madagascar, the beach was reputedly left strewn with unwanted luxuries such as silks, gold-embroidered muslins, and spices. This pirate captain and about 40 of his men then retired to the French island of Bourbon (later, Réunion), where they received a pardon from its Governor and settled down. According to legend, Condent later married this official's sister-in-law and emigrated to St-Malô, France, where he became a rich ship owner.

But whatever his eventual fate, Condent's good fortune certainly attracted other rovers. One of these proved to be another former New Providence man, the Welsh-born Howell Davis, who roamed the Guinea Coast of West Africa in 1719. At noon on 5 June (Old Style),

Davis had an unusually significant encounter when he stood into the English slaving station of Anamaboe, with his two ships. The first of these was described by an eye-witness as being the *King James*, a black-hulled vessel with a skull-and-crossbones fluttering from her mast-

Right: Contemporary woodcut of Edward England.

Right: A depiction of that cunning pirate commander, Howell Davis.

head; the other was a Dutch trader mounting 32 cannon and 27 swivels, which Davis had recently captured off Cape Three Points and renamed the *Royal Rover*. His pair quickly subdued and pillaged the three English slavers lying in the roads, even removing some of their prime seamen. Among the latter was the third mate of the merchant-galley *Princess* out of London, a skilled mariner in his late thirties named Bartholomew Roberts.

Six weeks later, Davis visited the Portuguese colony of Principe Island in the Guinea Gulf, masquerading as a Royal Naval officer seeking re-supply after a patrol against pirates. The local Portuguese Governor was not deceived, however, turning the tables by persuading Davis and a landing-party to come ashore, where they were ambushed and the Welshman slain. Retreating out to sea aboard the *Royal Rover*, his surviving crewmembers elected Roberts to fill his place, despite the latter's very brief experience among the pirates. Their new captain – despite never having served in any dishonest capacity – would prove an astonishingly resourceful corsair leader, and indeed the last of the great rover chieftains. Roberts himself later explained his willingness to embrace this disreputable new calling by saying:

> In an honest service there is thin rations, low wages and hard labour; in this [*i.e.*, roving], plenty and satiety, pleasure and ease, liberty and power; and who would not balance creditor on this side, when all the hazard that is run for it, at worst, is only a sour look or two at choking [*i.e.*, hanging]. No, a merry life and a short one shall be my motto.

Having committed himself to sail under the black flag, he added: 'It is better to be a commander than a common man, since I have dipped my hands in muddy waters and must be a pirate.'

'Black Bart', as he came to be known, would spend the next two and a half years on spectacular campaigns against both sides of the Atlantic. After first devastating Principe Island in retaliation for Davis's death, he swept through the Bight of Biafra before laying a course across the ocean toward Brazil. In September 1719, Roberts's ship came upon a Portuguese con-

voy of 42 merchantmen preparing to depart Bahia, escorted by two men-of-war. Sailing impudently into their midst, he plundered the wealthiest of 400,000 gold moidores, before retiring utterly unscathed.

The pirates then visited Devil's Island in the Guianas, before being chased further northward out of the Caribbean by Royal Naval patrols. Ranging as far as the south-eastern tip of Newfoundland, *Royal Rover* stood into Trepassey Bay in June 1720 with the Jolly Roger flying from her masthead, and the ship's band loudly playing on deck. An English merchant convoy of 22 sail was gathering within, whose crews fled ashore in panic while Roberts casually rifled their holds. *Royal Rover* being worn, he transferred into a Bristol galley which he renamed *Royal Fortune*. His audacity was so breath-taking that the Governor of New England could not refrain from concluding his report to London on this incident, with the comment: 'One cannot withhold admiration for his bravery and daring.'

Off the Grand Banks Roberts seized half-a-dozen French vessels, preferring one mounting 28 guns to his Bristol galley, and so moving his flag and giving this new ship the same name as her predecessor, *Royal Fortune*. Veering south-westwards, he then snapped up a string of prizes off New England in August 1720, the richest being the sloop *Samuel* out of London and bound for Boston. After ransacking her 'like a parcel of furies' (according to the *Boston News Letter*), Roberts's crew informed *Samuel*'s master:

We shall accept no Act of Grace, may the King and Parliament be damned with their Act of Grace for us, neither will we go to Hope Point [*i.e.,* Execution Dock] to be hanged a-sun-drying.

Instead they let it be known that they would only seek pardons when they had accumulated enough money, which they judged to be 'seven or eight hundred pounds each'.

In September *Royal Fortune* returned briefly to the West Indies, touching at Deseada Island in the Lesser Antilles for water before striking out across the Atlantic again towards Africa. Contrary winds so dogged this passage, though, that Roberts and his 124 men almost died of thirst before being driven back into Suriname, on the north coast of South America. Deciding to abandon all caution, Roberts gambled on rampaging through the Windward Islands, notwithstanding the presence of several Royal Naval patrols and the lack of any adequate pirate sanctuaries. His boldness was rewarded by dozens of prizes, the Governor of the French Leeward Islands noting at one point that: 'Between the 28th and 31st October [1720] these pirates seized, burned or sank fifteen French and English vessels and one Dutch interloper of 42 guns at Dominica.'

Basing himself off Saint Lucia, Roberts inflicted such a heavy toll on French shipping plying to and from Martinique that its Governor was forced to plead for help from the neighbouring British authorities. The Governor of Barbados attempted to assist his beleaguered French colleague, which co-operation so angered Roberts that he designed a special pirate jack, showing a figure of himself standing

Left: Bartholomew Roberts, the last great sea renegade, who was to enjoy a spectacular, but meteoric career.

with a sword in his right hand and each foot on a skull: one having the initials 'ABH' written beneath it, signifying 'A Barbadian's Head', the other 'AMH' for 'A Martinican's Head'. The plate on his cabin door also bore this same design.

By the spring of 1721 Roberts had nearly brought Antillean commerce to a standstill, and so prepared to sail away. Knowing he could expect to find no haven in American waters, he loaded all his plunder aboard two captured ships and struck out across the Atlantic that April, towards Sierra Leone. Here there existed a tiny outlaw colony of European smugglers and interlopers, who were not adverse to trading with pirates. One of its more famous shore establishments was run by an ex-buccaneer named John Leadstone, alias 'Old Crackers'; another on the Rio Pungo was maintained by Benjamin Gun, who would later serve as the model for Robert Louis Stevenson's 'Ben Gunn' in *Treasure Island*. Roberts spent six weeks here, before setting out eastward again in late August 1721. Off Sestos (in present-day Liberia) he captured the Royal African Company frigate *Onslow*, increasing its armament from 26 to 40 guns and converting it into his last *Royal Fortune*. Slowly continuing his way south-eastward, he eventually reached Cape Lopez at about

Christmas time, before reversing course north-westwards.

Roberts realised that there were two powerful Royal Naval warships patrolling that coastline, HMSS *Swallow* and *Weymouth*, each mounting 50 guns and almost brand-new, having been launched only two years previously. Believing that these had returned to their winter quarters off Sierra Leone, the pirate captain doubled back along his course and on Thursday, 11 January 1722 (Old Style), brashly stood into the great slaving port of Ouidah. Brushing aside its feeble defences, he sent boarding-parties aboard the eleven slavers lying in its roads and held these for ransom, demanding eight pounds of gold dust apiece (about £500 each, in the currency of the day). All agreed to pay, save one master whose ship, despite the 80 slaves fettered in its hold, was set on fire and sunk.

Two days later, however, Roberts intercepted a message from Cape Coast Castle to the Royal African Company's agent in Ouidah, warning him that the pirates were headed in his direction – with *Swallow* in close pursuit. Alarmed to learn that this Royal Navy vessel was so near at hand, Roberts immediately fled out to sea and headed south-eastward towards Cape Lopez again. Two days later *Swallow* entered Ouidah, and her commander, Captain Chaloner Ogle, made a

Above, left and right: 'Black Bart's' original standard showed him holding an hour-glass, together with an armed Death-figure. However, angered by the threatened cooperation between English and French authorities on Barbados and Martinique, he created a new flag with himself bestriding two skulls marked ABH and AMH, for 'A Barbadian's Head' and 'A Martinican's Head'.

shrewd guess as to the intruder's intended bolthole. Pressing on for Cape Lopez himself, the Royal Naval officer began searching its shoreline until at daybreak on 5 February 1722 (Old Style), he heard the sound of a lone gun being fired in the distance. Sailing in the direction of this noise, he at last spotted Roberts's trio of vessels lying at anchor beneath the Cape: *Royal Fortune* and her consorts *Great Ranger* and *Little Ranger*.

Aboard the pirate flagship, Roberts too saw this strange sail appear, and assumed it to be a large merchantman. Consequently he ordered his subordinate Captain James Skyrme to pursue with *Great Ranger*, while Ogle cunningly turned *Swallow* away at this same moment, running before the wind as if afraid, but actually allowing his single pursuer to overhaul. By 10.30 that morning Cape Lopez had fallen below the horizon, and Skyrme had closed sufficiently astern of *Swallow*

Right: Bartholomew Roberts's *Great Ranger* (left) and *Royal Fortune* bear down upon eleven anchored slavers at Ouidah, West Africa.

to open fire with his bow-chasers. The distance continued to narrow, and *Great Ranger*'s decks were lined with cutlass-brandishing pirates, while she displayed a bewildering array of flags – including, most prominently, a Jolly Roger.

Half an hour later Ogle decided to spring the trap by bearing up to starboard, running out his guns, and letting fly with a crushing broadside. The pirates were appalled to discover that they had been lured directly beneath the muzzles of a heavily armed man-of-war, and reacted with some confusion. A

brisk firefight ensued, in which one of Skyrme's legs was blown off, and *Great Ranger* lost her maintopmast. Finally by 3 o'clock that afternoon the pirates had had enough, and a desperately wounded Skyrme struck his colours and cast these into the sea, so that they could not be used in evidence against him in a court of law. Meanwhile half-a-dozen of his most desperate crew-members ran down into *Great Ranger*'s magazine, where they stuck a pistol into a barrel of gunpowder and pulled the trigger, so as to blow everyone aboard into oblivion. This container proved to be only partially full, however, so that while the would-be suicides were terribly burnt, their ship did not explode or sink.

Thus when *Swallow*'s boarders came over her bulwarks, they found

ten pirates dead and another twenty wounded, out of a crew of one hundred men: 59 of them British, eighteen French, and the rest Africans. The Royal Navy warship had not suffered a single casualty. Ogle temporarily repaired *Great Ranger* and sent her limping back towards Principe Island with her wounded pirates under guard, while the uninjured captives were clapped below decks aboard *Swallow* to return to Cape Lopez. Ogle came within sight of this headland again on the morning of 10 February (Old Style), just as Roberts was sitting in *Royal Fortune*'s great cabin finishing off his favourite breakfast dish of *salmigondis*. The rover was neither worried by *Great Ranger*'s five-day absence, nor by the approach of this strange ship under a French flag. It

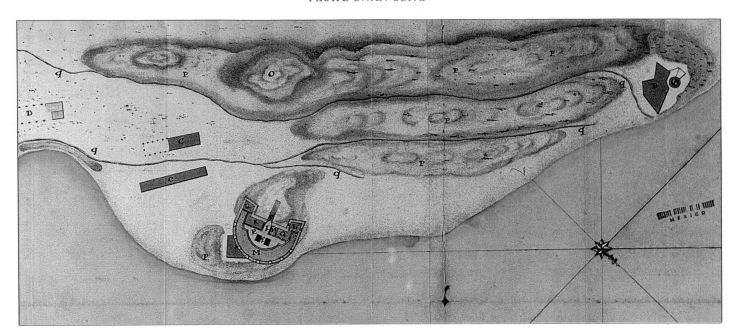

Above and opposite page: Map and detail of the new Spanish coastal battery erected at Mocambo, Veracruz. Scores of such small defences were erected throughout the Caribbean, gradually denying the buccaneers their favourite observation points, sanctuaries, and disembarkation places for land raids. (Archivo General de la Nación, Mexico)

Left: The pirate Edward Low's ship foundering in a storm.

was only when *Swallow* had drawn close enough to be plainly visible from on deck that one of the pirates – a naval deserter who had previously served aboard this man-of-war – recognised his former ship and cried a warning.

Belatedly, Roberts sprang into action, coming on deck and ordering *Little Ranger*'s crew to reinforce *Royal Fortune*, thus bringing his flagship's strength to 152 men. At 10.30 he slipped his cable and got under way, directing full sail be set. As *Royal Fortune* gathered way, her commander ducked below and put on his finery in anticipation of a battle. He returned wearing a crimson waistcoat and breeches, and a hat with a large red feather in it.

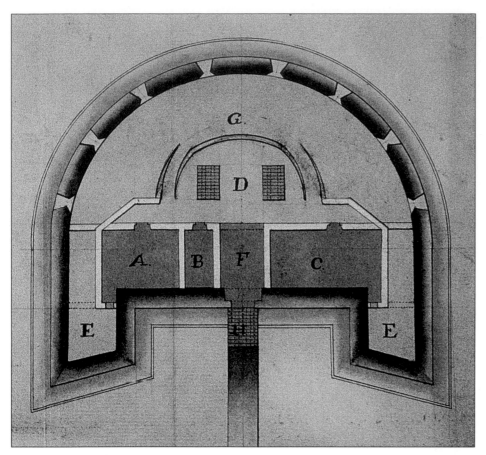

From his neck dangled numerous gold chains and a silk sling, with two pairs of pistols thrust through it. Gaining his poop deck, Roberts then inexplicably altered course directly towards *Swallow*, and at 11 o'clock leapt on to a gun-carriage to begin directing his ship's artillery.

But it was the man-of-war which boomed out the first rounds, bringing *Royal Fortune*'s mizzentopmast crashing down with a single well-aimed broadside. When the smoke and wreckage was cleared, the pirates discovered Roberts draped over the rope tackles of one of the guns, dead from a wound to his throat. He was not quite forty years of age. Greatly distressed at the death of their brilliant captain, his followers quickly cast his body into the sea (in accordance with his oft-expressed wishes), then fought on as best they could, hoping to win free. However, without Roberts they were no match for *Swallow*, which continued to pound *Royal Fortune*

relentlessly until 1.30 in the afternoon, when the pirates' mainmast collapsed. By 2 o'clock they were begging for quarter, and Ogle sent over his boarders, who secured the prisoners and carried them into the English slave factory of Cape Coast Castle to stand trial.

Eventually 52 of these pirates were condemned to hang, twenty to serve as manual labourers in the Royal African Company's gold-mines (which sentence none survived), seventeen to transportation to Marshalsea Prison in London (only four reaching this destination alive), while the 76 others were either acquitted or reprieved. Such numbers were totally insignificant when measured against the tens of thousands of sailors serving at sea, yet Roberts's demise marked a distinct watershed in the history of piracy.

Half a century earlier his intelligence, charisma and courage might have earned him a knighthood,

such as Morgan and De Graaf had received, or at least offers of wartime command and a comfortable, honourable retirement ashore. Instead his meteoric rise had seen him chased to the far ends of the earth, with every government's hand raised against him. Despite having captured more than four hundred vessels during his spectacular career, this success had not led to either financial or social reward. He ended his days in a watery grave, leaving lesser marauders to ponder what their own fate must be, where such a talented leader as Roberts had failed. Indeed, it was Ogle who received the knighthood, from a country grateful that he had slain this hated pirate.

The rovers now continued to shift their dwindling operations even farther afield, reviving their depredations in the Indian Ocean. As has already been noted, the pirate lairs on Madagascar had been largely abandoned during the late 1690s, following Baldridge's retirement from Saint Mary's, and the arrival of Commodore Warren's squadron of four Royal Naval warships into South African waters. The latter cruised off this particular island for the better part of a year, their mere presence succeeding in driving away the remaining pirates. Madagascar did not become a marauder outpost again for another twenty years, when this last wave of refugee buccaneers began to appear, under such commanders as England and Condent.

By 1720, a rover named John Plantain had set up a base on Madagascar very similar to the one established by Baldridge 45 years previously. Plantain was born at Chocolate Hole, Jamaica, and first went to sea at the age of thirteen. By the time he turned twenty he was a fully fledged pirate serving aboard a Rhode Island-based sloop named *Terrible*. After rounding the Cape of Good Hope and spending a couple of seasons successfully plundering

a second pirate ship – John Taylor's *Victory* – suddenly materialised behind the first, at which point *Greenwich* slipped out of the bay, leaving Macrae to face both marauder vessels alone. 'He basely deserted us,' *Cassandra*'s captain later complained to his directors, 'and left us engaged with barbarous and inhuman enemies with their black and bloody flags hanging over us, and no appearance of escaping being cut to pieces.'

Nevertheless Macrae put up a stout resistance, fighting off the two pirate ships for the next three or four hours. By 4 o'clock in the afternoon, though, it became apparent that he had suffered too many casualties to be able to repel his enemies much longer. Macrae therefore headed *Cassandra* inshore, hoping to beach her and at least allow his crew to escape on land. *Fancy* pursued, and both vessels ran aground in the shallows, exchanging heavy gunfire. But as England's ship had become hung up with its bows exposed to *Cassandra*'s broadside, he was forced to beg three additional boatloads of men from Taylor's *Victory*, before the latter finally put an end to the battle by towing his ship directly beneath the East Indiaman's stern. Macrae reluctantly ordered his men into the boats, and by 7 o'clock that evening had all his survivors ashore, leaving behind thirteen dead and 24 wounded.

The pirates took possession of their hard-won prize with its £75,000 worth of trade goods, then offered a bounty of two thousand pounds for the person of Macrae himself. This brave captain, though, of his own volition ventured aboard the pirate ships ten days later – once their fighting fury had abated – to negotiate a way off the island for himself and his men. Impressed by his courage, England gave him the badly damaged *Fancy* and those

in the Gulf of Aden, Plantain retired to Ranter Bay on Madagascar, a harbour located just north of Baldridge's former base of Saint Mary's. Here Plantain and two other pirate chieftains – a Scot named James Adair and a Dane named Hans Burgen – built a stockaded fortress complete with a sumptuous harem, from which they traded with all passing ships. Plantain styled himself the 'King of Ranter Bay', and cowed the local tribesmen with his arsenal of European firearms. Although short-lived, this last burst of pirate glory was to wit-

ness some memorable coups, before the inevitable dispersal.

In August of 1720, for example, the British East Indiamen *Cassandra* commanded by Captain James Macrae, and *Greenwich* under Captain Richard Kirby, put into Johanna Island near Madagascar for water. While preparing to stand out of harbour again, they saw Edward England's pirate ship *Fancy* bearing down on them, 'flying a black flag at the maintopmast, a red flag at the foretopmast, and the cross of Saint George at the ensign staff'. *Cassandra* immediately engaged, but then trade items which the pirates did not want, permitting the merchant master and his crew to sail away. After a terrible 48-day ordeal, Macrae succeeded in reaching the East India Company's factory in India, where he was promoted and eventually rose to become Governor of Madras.

Meanwhile his opponent England had suffered a distinctly different fate, despite his triumph. Enraged at the heavy casualties they had endured capturing an outward-bound vessel without any Oriental treasure on board, his minions vented their disgust by voting England out as captain. Furthermore they banished him from their company, giving him and his few adherents a small boat with which they reached Saint Augustine's Bay on Madagascar, where England died in abject poverty soon afterwards. Taylor now assumed overall command of the remaining band, setting sail with the captured *Cassandra* to make one last great haul in the waning days of piracy.

On Quasimodo Sunday, 26 April 1721, he stood into the roadstead of Saint Denis on the island of Bourbon (Réunion) in the Mauritius island group, accompanied by the French corsair vessel *Victoire* of Capitaine La Buze. Inside they found the Portuguese East Indiaman *Nossa Senhora do Cabo* ('Our Lady of the Cape') undergoing repairs, having become dismasted in a gale during her homeward passage from Goa, India. Thus this vessel was heavy laden with the expected luxuries of the Orient, plus an enormous consignment of diamonds destined for the Portuguese royal family, as well as others belonging to the retiring Viceroy of Goa, Dom Luis Carlos Ignacio Xavier de Meneses, fifth Count of Ericeira, who was also on board.

The Portuguese vessel at first prepared to salute these two strange ships once they dropped anchor, as was customary, but these continued to advance straight into the harbour until they ranged up on each side of the *Cabo*, then struck their false British colours and substituted black flags with white skull-and-crossbones. At this moment each let fly with a thunderous broadside, and the Portuguese Indiaman found itself sore beset. Only 21 of her guns

Edward England's pirate flag

were mounted, and there were only 34 muskets aboard for her 130-man crew. The pirates totalled almost twice this number, and were so much better armed that they naturally chose to board, rather than exchange broadsides. Grenades were hurled on to *Cabo*'s deck and the pirates swarmed howling over her bulwarks, while the crew fled below. Alone on the quarter-deck, the Count of Ericeira slashed at the marauders until his sword blade broke, being spared when Taylor roared above the din for quarter to be given, and all fighting ceased.

Ericeira's courage at least won the pirates' respect, and they returned his broken sword to him, although its hilt was richly encrusted with gold and diamonds. They offered to restore some of his personal effects as well, when the French Governor of that island ransomed him, but

the Portuguese nobleman proudly refused, only to watch in horror as his priceless Oriental manuscripts and books were torn up to make wadding and cartridges for the pirates' guns. Taylor and his companions remained ecstatic, for the diamonds aboard *Cabo* were worth upwards of £500,000; the silks, porcelain and other goods another £375,000. Added to the plunder which the pirates had already accrued during their cruise, the total came to more than a million pounds. At the final share-out, each of the pirates received more than £4,000, plus 42 small diamonds per man. (One of the rovers received a single large diamond reckoned to be the equivalent of 42 small ones, which he smashed to bits in a mortar, believing it worth more in fragments than as a whole.)

Now at last immensely rich men, the pirates decided to retire from their wanderings on the sea. Some accepted a French pardon and settled on the island of Bourbon, others chose to live on Madagascar. The remainder, about 140 Englishmen and New Englanders, sailed back around the Cape of Good Hope and into the Caribbean. Here they attempted to purchase a pardon from the Governor of Jamaica, but were refused, so in July 1723 dropped anchor in the Spanish-American port of Portobelo. Because of their dazzling wealth, they were able to buy a pardon from the local authorities, and in one final touch of irony concluded their piratical careers by stepping on to its oft-ravaged beaches as free men. Taylor, the last truly successful pirate, was to spend the rest of his days as a well-to-do Spanish *guardacosta* officer, commanding a patrol vessel in the same waters once set a-tremble by such ghostly precursors as John Coxon and Henry Morgan.

Pirate Rules

Seventeenth-century buccaneer raids, especially such massive enterprises as Morgan's campaign against Panama (which involved more than two thousand freebooters of many different nationalities), required a prior written understanding as to conditions of service and the eventual division of spoils, both in order to inform its participants, as well as to avoid later disputes. These covenants were often called 'charter-parties' by the British, derived from the French commercial term *charte-partie*, used when two or more merchants agreed to share a hired vessel.

If only a single merchant were involved, the question of cargo space was not a pressing concern; but in the case of a *charte-partie* (literally, 'split charter'), each consignor's portion had to be carefully allotted. Thus the French *flibustiers* – many of whom were veteran merchant sailors – adopted this expression to their own affairs, whence it passed into English. The typical buccaneer charter spelt out the expected code of conduct for the forthcoming campaign, with punishments for infractors, plus special clauses for the compensation of wounded, senior commanders, specialists, etc.

They also had a certain legal status, such as when Morgan was threatened with a law-suit in late September 1671 by a Jamaican physician named Dr George Holmes, for the loss of the latter's 50-ton sloop *Port Royal* outside Chagres during the Panama expedition. Holmes demanded £300 in compensation, pointing out that such payments were recognised by the freebooters' own charter, and that Morgan himself had received £1,000 for the wreck of his 120-ton *Satisfaction* during this same incident. When Morgan at first refused to comply, Holmes requested that the Council of Jamaica summon him to a hearing, at which a decision could be rendered 'as shall be agreeable to law

Left: A drunken *boucanier* celebration.

and equity'. This was never convened, Morgan apparently preferring to settle out of court.

But by the early eighteenth century, as the buccaneers' large-scale land forays gradually diminished in favour of piracy, the rovers' charters also underwent a change, becoming more like secret covenants than public documents. Indeed, pirates were even at some pains to destroy these papers if in danger of capture, because they realised that these could be entered against them in a court of law. One of the few sets of pirate articles to survive was that sworn by the followers of Bartholomew Roberts, when he was unexpectedly killed off the West African coast in February 1722. These stipulated that:

I. Every man shall have an equal vote in affairs of moment. He shall have an equal title to the fresh provisions or strong liquors at any time seized, and shall use them at pleasure unless a scarcity may make it necessary for the common good that a retrenchment may be voted.

II. Every man shall be called fairly in turn by the list on board of prizes, because over and above their proper share, they are allowed a shift of clothes. But if they defraud the company to the value of even one dollar in plate, jewels or money, they shall be marooned. If any man rob another he shall have his nose and ears slit, and be put ashore where he shall be sure to encounter hardships.

III. None shall game for money either with dice or cards.

IV. The lights and candles should be put out at eight at night, and if any of the crew desire to drink after that hour they shall sit upon the open deck without lights.

V. Each man shall keep his piece, cutlass and pistols at all times clean and ready for action.

VI. No boy or woman to be allowed amongst them. If any man shall be found seducing any of the latter sex and carrying her to sea in disguise, he shall suffer death.

VII. He that shall desert the ship or his quarters in time of battle shall be punished by death or marooning.

VIII. None shall strike another on board the ship, but every man's quarrel shall be ended on shore by sword or pistol in this manner: at the word of command from the quartermaster, each man being previously placed back to back, shall turn and fire immediately. If any man do not, the quartermaster shall knock the piece out of his hand. If both miss their aim, they shall take to their cutlasses, and he that draws first blood shall be declared the victor.

IX. No man shall talk of breaking up their way of living till each has a share of £1,000. Every man who shall become a cripple or lose a limb in the service shall have eight hundred pieces of eight from the common stock, and for lesser hurts proportionately.

X. The captain and the quartermaster shall each receive two shares of a prize, the master gunner and boatswain, one and one half shares, all other officers one and one quarter, and private gentlemen of fortune [*i.e.*, seamen] one share each.

XI. The musicians shall have rest on the Sabbath Day only, by right; on all other days, by favour only.

Epilogue

Arise, ye more than dead.
John Dryden (1631–1700)

Piracy would continue to smoulder for many more decades, of course, even centuries, right up to our present day. The age-old inhumanity of the strong preying upon the weak has never really ceased to exist upon the high seas, any more than it has on dry land. Rich merchants and poor fishermen alike sailed the oceans with a certain trepidation, always keeping a weather eye on the horizon for any dark, threatening silhouette.

But the days when outlaw bands roamed the waves with insolent pride, descending upon any hapless coastal region to sack and pillage at will, had become a thing of the past. Around the globe, Europe's colonies were growing increasingly stable and prosperous, and no longer dependent upon privateers for their security. Instead they now regarded these as an impediment to good trade, and so gradually eradicated them. Henceforth, major anti-piracy campaigns would consist of wars against all enemies of free commerce, often directed against local native sailors

Left: French seamen defend their ship ferociously against pirates in the Far East.

Above: Destruction of the Wahabi Gulf pirate lairs of Ras al Khaymah, by an English expedition in November 1809.

who terrorised international sea-traffic in their areas.

One such confrontation developed in the Arabian Sea, when one of the ships of the Maratha Admiral Kanhoji Angria was seized by the British East India Company in 1718, while peacefully employed in the harbour at Bombay. Although originally a mountainous people from the Western Ghats, the Marathas had expanded until they controlled a number of small coastal kingdoms below Bombay, as far south as Goa.

They had frequently clashed with the British factors before, over the rights to control and levy taxes on the merchant shipping passing through their waters. A treaty had been signed five years previously, whereby the Marathas had agreed not to bother the Company's ships, but this soon foundered over different interpretations of what constituted such a vessel, plus the fact that the Company began selling licences to any ship master willing to pay their price.

Incensed at the loss of his ship, Angria threatened reprisals, at which the East India Company Governor in Bombay, Charles Boone, attempted a series of assaults against the string of stone Maratha fortresses stretching away southward from that city. These ended in failure, the siege of Gheriah in 1721

being particularly ignominious, when the British attempted to batter down its walls with an unwieldy, heavily protected floating battery called the *Prahm*. This proved so clumsy that it was finally towed out to sea and unceremoniously burnt, after which an uneasy stalemate ensued with the Marathas until Angria's death in 1729.

After a brief succession struggle among his sons, hostilities resumed. In 1735 the East Indiaman *Derby* was captured after a half-hearted resistance, and taken into the Maratha stronghold of Severndroog. This ship proved a valuable prize, for not only did she contain the annual shipment of English gold for Bombay, but also a large supply of ammunition and naval stores, which helped reinvigorate Maratha strength. Such intercep-

tions continued throughout the 1740s under the leadership of Tulaji Angria, son and successor to Kanhoji.

The turning-point in British fortunes at last came in the person of William James of the Bombay Marine. James had been commander of the *Guardian*, built by the East India Company in 1751 to protect its Malabar trade, and by 1755 he had decided to confront the Angrians head-on. Backed by a small squadron of four ships, he brought his 40-gun flagship *Protector* so close under the fort at Severndroog that few of its guns could be depressed to bear upon his vessel, then subjected this castle to a steady bombardment over the next two days which culminated in the explosion of its magazine and surrender of the garrison.

In February 1756 the major remaining fort at Gheriah was taken by a combined operation, in which the land forces were led by Robert Clive, and the Bombay navy by James. For his singular role in thus helping break the Angrian stranglehold over British trade, James received a government award which enabled him to retire to England, on a farm near Eltham in Kent. On nearby Shooter's Hill, his widow eventually erected a memorial tower known as 'Severndroog Castle' which stands to this day and:

> ... records the achievements of the brave,
> and Angria's subjugated power who plundered on the eastern wave.

By the 1760s, most piracy had shifted to the islands at the mouth of China's Canton River, which became a popular new destination for European traders. These islands (including the future Hong Kong) were named the Ladrones, from the

Above: Chinese pirate attack on a European vessel, near present-day Hong Kong.

Portuguese word for robber or brigand.

Towards the end of the eighteenth century, attacks on European merchantmen began to multiply in these waters, and the beginning of the nineteenth century saw the amalgamation of its pirates into a gigantic combine under a brilliant leader named Ching Yih. By 1805 he almost completely dominated the coast around Canton, his forces totalling five or six hundred vessels, the largest being junks mounting twelve guns apiece. His fleet was divided into six squadrons, each with its distinctively coloured flag, and allotted different areas to cruise for prey. Trading vessels that purchased a licence were suffered to pass by all squadrons, but any others were boarded and robbed. Resistance meant the slaughter or enslavement of the crews.

Even the appearance two years later of the Royal Navy's 74-gun ship-of-the-line *Bellona* and the frigate *Phaeton* failed to intimidate these hardened rovers, as was amply demonstrated in an incident observed by one English officer:

> About sixty or seventy sail of Ladrones passed in the most impudent manner within range of the guns ... Determined to punish the presumption of these pirates, the frigate opened a smart fire on them, which was received by the Ladrones with the utmost coolness and indifference, and without even returning a shot.

Ching Yih died in a typhoon in 1807, but was succeeded by his even more remarkable widow Ching Yih Saou, who became commonly known as Ching Shih, and greatly enhanced the rovers' power. Several Ladrone junks already had female captains, and Ching Shih proved to be an exceptionally diligent admiral. Her code of conduct included the following rules:

> No pirate might go ashore without permission. Punishment for a first offence was perforation of the ears; a repetition attracted the death penalty.

> All plundered goods must be registered before distribution. The ship responsible for the taking of a particular piece of booty received a fifth of its value, the remainder became part of the general fund.

> Abuse of women was forbidden (although women were taken

Right: Asian boarders swarm aboard a nineteenth-century European vessel.

as slaves and concubines). Those not kept for ransom were sold to the pirates as wives for $40 each.

> Country people were to be paid for provisions and stores taken from them.

Soon she had a fleet of eight hundred large junks, nearly one thousand smaller boats, and a pirate throng of 70–80,000 men and women under her command. The largest of her war junks weighed 600 tons, mounted 30 guns and carried three to four hundred men. This was the flagship of the Red Squadron, chief among the divisions of her fleet, which was as large as the other five put together.

Such a formidable host naturally paralysed traffic along the south China coast, yet required a constant stream of victims in order to survive. On 1 October 1809, Ching Shih even led a disembarkation against the villages west of Bocca Tigris, torching whole settlements and kidnapping or massacring their inhabitants. But soon afterwards, her favourite lieutenant (and reputed lover) Chang Paou, fell out with the commander of Black Squadron, Kwo Po Tai, and their two forces clashed in a savage battle off Lantao. Many junks were blown up with everyone on board, while others continued to resist so long as there was still a single man left to fight.

Eventually Chang Paou withdrew from these bloodied waters, conceding victory to the upstart Kwo Po Tai; however, the latter quickly appreciated the weakness of his new position, and offered his services to the Chinese imperial government. Created a naval mandarin, he returned into the South China Sea with a commission to hunt pirates, and when Ching Shih and Chang Paou learnt of this, they too opted to retire from the sea.

In 1810 her fleet sailed upriver towards Bocca Tigris, with all flags flying. At Canton they surrendered, and by the terms of the treaty Chang Paou was also appointed to the rank of naval mandarin, with orders to hunt the remaining pirates of Yellow and Green Squadrons, while the woman admiral Ching Shih withdrew from roving altogether. As with every other previous major pirate enterprise, this one too had eventually succumbed – in no small part because of its very success, outgrowing its ability to support so many participants, while at the same time lacking adequate resources ashore.

A similar fate awaited the Barbary States a few years later, on the far side of the globe. At the conclusion of the Napoleonic Wars, a combined Anglo–Dutch fleet commanded by Admiral Lord Exmouth (formerly Sir Edward Pellew) bombarded Algiers in August 1816, to protest against the corsairs' continual policy of intercepting passing Mediterranean merchantmen to enslave their crews. After inflicting extensive damage, some 3,000 captives were freed, and other punitive expeditions followed against both Tunis and Tripoli. Finally the French invaded Algeria in 1830, effectively putting an end to piracy in that particular corner of the world.

During Victoria's long reign, the once fearful rovers were at last reduced to utter impotence, an insignificant factor on seas ruled by ever more modern battle fleets, which only a powerful nation could maintain. Steam, advanced ballistics, telegraphic communications and other technological innovations meant that the advantage swung decisively to the professional services. Whereas in Drake's day, or even Morgan's, a naval warship and privateer might meet on something like equal terms, by the late nineteenth century this disparity had become insurmountable. No longer did mercenaries command respect, while even the tiniest ironclad could remorselessly hunt down any renegade, or decimate a raider fleet, or smoke out a hidden lair. The tide had run its course, and now it was the pirates' turn to fear.

Select Bibliography

A. General Books

One of the best bibliographies dealing with piracy is the *'Piracy and Privateering'* catalogue of the National Maritime Museum Library, Volume Four (London: Her Majesty's Stationery Office, 1972), which contains a wealth of detail on many printed historical sources. Collections of published documents are also extremely valuable, including:

Calendar of State Papers, Colonial Series, America and West Indies. London: Her Majesty's Stationery Office, 1860–1969, 44 vols.

Interesting Tracts Relating to the Island of Jamaica, Consisting of Curious State Papers, Councils of War, Letters, Petitions, Narratives, etc., Which Throw Great Light on the History of that Island from its Conquest down to the Year 1702. St Jago de la Vega (Kingston, Jamaica): Lewis, Lunan and Jones, 1800.

Jameson, John Franklin. *Privateering and Piracy in the Colonial Period: Illustrative Documents*. New York: Macmillan, 1923.

Some English-language editions that deal with piracy and privateering on a broad scope are:

Barbour, Violet F. 'Privateers and Pirates of the West Indies' in *American Historical Review*, vol. XVI (1911), pp. 529–66.

Bensusan, Harold G. 'The Spanish Struggle Against Foreign Encroachment in the Caribbean, 1675–1697.' Unpublished Ph.D. thesis, University of California at Los Angeles, 1970.

Botting, Douglas. *The Pirates*. Alexandria, Virginia. Time-Life Books, 1978.

Bromley, John Selwyn. *Corsairs and Navies, 1660–1760*. London: Hambledon, 1988.

Carr, H. Gresham. 'Pirate Flags', in *The Mariner's Mirror* (1943), pp. 131–4.

Chapin, Howard Millar. *Privateer Ships and Sailors: The First Century of American Colonial Privateering, 1625–1725*. Toulon: G. Mouton, 1926.

Cordingly, David, and Falconer, John. *Pirates*. New York: Abbeville Press, 1992.

Dow, George Francis, and Edmonds, John Henry. *The Pirates of the New England Coast, 1630–1730*. Salem: Marine Research Society, 1923.

Fuller, Basil, and Leslie-Melville, Ronald. *Pirate Harbours and their Secrets*. London: Stanley Paul, 1935.

Galvin, Peter R. 'The Pirates' Wake: A Geography of Piracy and Pirates as Geographers in Colonial Spanish America, 1536–1718.' Unpublished Ph.D. thesis, Louisiana State University, 1991.

Gerhard, Peter. *Pirates on the West Coast of New Spain, 1575–1742*. Glendale, California: Arthur H. Clark, 1960.

Gosse, Dr Philip Henry George. *The Pirates' Who's Who*. London: Dulau, 1924.

— *My Pirate Library*. London: Dulau, 1926.

— *A Bibliography of the Works of Capt. Charles Johnson*. London: Dulau, 1927.

— *The History of Piracy*. London: Longmans Green, 1932.

— 'Piracy', in *The Mariner's Mirror*, vol. XXXVI (1950), pp. 337–49.

Haring, Clarence Henry. *The Buccaneers in the West Indies in the XVII Century*. London: Methuen, 1910.

Hussey, R. D. 'Spanish Reaction to Foreign Aggression in the Caribbean to about 1680', in *Hispanic American Historical Review*, vol. 9 (1929), pp. 286–302.

Margolin, Samuel G. 'Lawlessness on the Maritime Frontier of the Greater Chesapeake, 1650–1750 (Smuggling, Wrecking, Piracy).' Unpublished Ph.D. thesis, College of William and Mary, 1992.

Marley, David F. *Pirates and Privateers of the Americas*. Santa Barbara, California, and Oxford, England: ABC–Clio, 1994.

Mitchell, David. *Pirates*. London: Thames & Hudson, 1976.

Rediker, Marcus. *Between the Devil and the Deep Blue Sea: Merchant Seamen, Pirates and the Anglo–American Maritime World, 1700–1750*. Cambridge: Cambridge University Press, 1987.

Shomette, Donald G. *Pirates on the Chesapeake: Being a True History of Pirates, Picaroons, and Raiders on Chesapeake Bay, 1610–1807*. Centreville, Maryland: 1985.

Ward, Eliot D. C. 'Imperial Panama: Commerce and Conflict in Isthmian America, 1550–1750.' Unpublished Ph.D. thesis, University of Florida, 1988.

Zahedieh, Nuala. '"A Frugal, Prudential and Hopeful Trade": Privateering in Jamaica, 1655–89', in *Journal of Imperial and Commonwealth History*, vol. 18, No. 2 (1990), pp. 145–68.

A great deal of excellent research has also been conducted by Spanish historians, whose people were often victimised by piratical depredations. Some of their more noteworthy contributions include:

Alsedo y Herrera, Dionisio de. *Piraterías y agresiones de los ingleses y de otros pueblos de Europa en la América Española desde el siglo XVI al XVIII*. Madrid: Manuel G. Hernández, 1883.

Calderón Quijano, José Ignacio. *Historia de las fortificaciones en Nueva España*. Seville: Escuela de Estudios Hispano–americanos, 1953.

Eugenio Martínez, María Angeles. *La defensa de Tabasco, 1600–1717*. Seville: Escuela de Estudios Hispano–americanos, 1971.

Garmendia Arruabarrena, José. 'Armadores y armadas de Guipúzcoa (1689–1692)', in *Boletín de Estudios Históricos de San Sebastián*. San Sebastián: Biblioteca de la Sociedad Bascongada de los Amigos del País, 1985, pp. 259–77.

Juárez Moreno, Juan. *Piratas y corsarios en Veracruz y Campeche*. Seville: Escuela de Estudios Hispano–americanos, 1972.

Lugo, Américo. *Recopilación diplomática relativa a las colonias española y francesa de la isla de Santo Domingo, 1640–1701*. Ciudad Trujillo, Dominican Republic: Editorial 'La Nación', 1944.

Peña Batlle, Manuel Arturo. *La isla de la Tortuga: Plaza de armas, refugio y seminario de los enemigos de España en Indias*. Madrid: Ediciones Cultura Hispánica, 1951.

Rubio Mañé, José Ignacio. 'Ocupación de la Isla de Términos por los ingleses, 1658–1717', in *Boletín del Archivo General de la Nación* [Mexico], Primera Serie, vol. XXIV, No. 2 (April–June 1953), pp. 295–330.

Sáiz Cidoncha, Carlos. *Historia de la piratería en América Española*. Madrid: Editorial San Martín, 1985.

Torres Ramírez, Bibiano. *La Armada de Barlovento*. Seville: Escuela de Estudios Hispano–americanos, 1981.

Significant French-language works include:

Buchet, Christian. *La lutte pour l'espace caraïbe et la façade atlantique de l'Amérique centrale et du Sud (1672–1763)*. Paris: Librairie de l'Inde, 1991.

Lepers, Jean–Baptiste. *La tragique histoire des Flibustiers: Histoire de Saint-Domingue et de l'Île de la Tortue, repairs des flibustiers, écrite vers 1715* (ed. Pierre–Bernard Berthelot). Paris: G. Crès, 1925.

Saint–Yves, G. 'La flibuste et les flibustiers. Documents inédits sur Saint Domingue et la Tortue', in *Bulletin de la Société de Géographie de Paris*, vol. 38 (1923), pp. 57–75.

It should be noted that the *Cahiers de Louis-Adhémar-Timothée Le Golif, dit 'Borgnefesse,' Capitaine de la Flibuste*, published in Paris by B. Grasset in 1952 (translated into English two years later by Allen & Unwin in London, under the title *Memoirs of a Buccaneer*), are now regarded as a forgery.

An interesting article in German is:

Hasenclever, Adolf. 'Die flibustier Westindiens im 17 jahrhundert', in *Preussische Jahrbuch*, vol. CCIII (1926), pp. 13–35.

B. Pirate Chroniclers

There also exist accounts left by several rovers, and their contemporaries, such as:

Dampier, William. *A New Voyage Round the World*. New York: Dover, 1968.

Ducéré, E. *Journal de bord d'un flibustier (1686–1693)*. Bayonne, 1894.

Exquemelin, Alexandre Olivier. *The Buccaneers of America*. Trans. from the Dutch by Alexis Brown, with an introduction by Jack Beeching. London: Penguin, 1969.

Gage, Thomas. *Thomas Gage's Travels in the New World*. (ed. J. Eric S. Thompson.) Norman, Oklahoma: University of Oklahoma Press, 1958.

Guijo, Gregorio M. de. *Diario, 1648–1664*. Mexico City: Editorial Porrúa, 1952, two vols.

Labat, Jean-Baptiste. *Viajes a las islas de la América*. Havana: Casa de las Américas, 1979.

Lussan, Ravenau de. *Journal of a Voyage into the South Seas*. Cleveland, Ohio: Arthur H. Clark Co., 1930.

Robles, Antonio de. *Diario de sucesos notables (1665–1703)*. Mexico City: Editorial Porrúa, 1972, three vols.

Sigüenza y Góngora, Carlos de. *Infortunios que Alonso Ramírez, natural de la ciudad de San Juan de Puerto Rico, padeció*. Repr. in *Obras históricas* (Mexico City: Porrúa, 1960).

Vrijman, L. C. *Dr David van der Sterre: Zeer aenmerkelijke reysen door Jan Erasmus Reyning*. Amsterdam: P. N. van Kampen & Zoon, 1937.

Wafer, Lionel. *A New Voyage and Description of the Isthmus of America*. London: Hakluyt Society, 1933.

Specific studies on these chroniclers themselves include:

Auffret, Pierre-Jean. 'Le Père Labat: "critique sous toutes les formes, il n'a que peu de temps à vivre", 1663–1738', in Lyon: *Documents pour Servir à l'Histoire de Saint Domingue en France*, 1973, 8:11–24.

Blanc, Gérard. 'Dampier, ou la relation des îles aux tortues', in *Dix-huitième siècle*, vol. 22 (1990), pp. 159–70.

Camus, Michel-Christian. 'Une note critique à propos d'Exquemelin', in *Revue française d'histoire d'outre-mer*, vol. 77, No. 286 (1990), pp. 79–90.

Harvey, John H. 'Some Notes on the Family of Dampier', in *The Mariner's Mirror*, vol. XXIX (1943), pp. 54–7.

Howse, Derek, and Thrower, Norman J. W., eds. *A Buccaneer's Atlas: Basil Ringrose's South Sea Waggoner. A Sea Atlas and Sailing Directions of the Pacific Coast of the Americas 1682*. Berkeley: University of California Press, 1992.

Le Pelley, John. 'Dampier's Morgan and the Privateersmen', in *The Mariner's Mirror*, vol. XXXIII (1947), pp. 170–8.

Lloyd, Christopher. *William Dampier*. London: Faber & Faber, 1966.

Poirier, M. 'Une grande figure antillaise: le R. P. Labat, aventurier, aumônier de la flibuste', in Nice: *Annales de la Société des Lettres, Sciences et Arts des Alpes–Maritimes*, vol. 61 (1969–70), pp. 83–94.

Young, Everild, and Helweg-Larsen, Kjeld. *The Pirates' Priest: The Life of Père Labat in the West Indies, 1693–1705*. London: Jarrolds, 1965.

C. Individual Events

Early conflicts involving seventeenth–century pirates in the West Indies are described in:

'Ataque y saqueo del puerto de Alvarado por piratas holandeses y franceses. (1651)', in *Boletín del Archivo General de la Nación* [Mexico], Primera Serie, vol. XXIV, No. 3 (July–September 1953), pp. 501–8.

Lepart, Jean. 'François Le Vasseur, de Cogners au Maine, capitaine flibustier et roi de l'Ile de la Tortue en 1652', in Le Mans: *La Province du Maine*, (October–December 1973), pp. 342–54.

Marley, David F. *Pirates and Engineers: Dutch and Flemish Adventurers in New Spain (1607–1697)*. Windsor, Ontario, Canada: Netherlandic Press, 1992.

Moya Pons, Frank. *Historia colonial de Santo Domingo*. Santiago, Dominican Republic: Universidad Católica Madre y Maestra, 1977.

Richard, Robert. 'A la Tortue et à Saint Domingue en 1649', in Seville: *Anuario de Estudios Americanos*, vol. 29 (1972), pp. 445–67.

Richard, Robert, and Débien, Gabriel. 'A la Tortue, après la mort de Le Vasseur (1652–53).' Le Mans: *La Province du Maine*, Vol. 81, No. 32 (Oct.–Dec. 1979), pp. 396–405.

Rodríguez Demorizi, Emilio. *La era de Francia en Santo Domingo; contribución a su estudio*. Ciudad Trujillo: Editora del Caribe, 1955.

The British conquest of Jamaica, and the round of hostilities against Spanish America which immediately followed, are described in:

Buisseret, David J. 'Edward D'Oyley, 1617–1675', in *Jamaica Journal* (1971), pp. 6–10.

Dyer, Florence E. 'Captain Christopher Myngs in the West Indies, 1657–1662', in *The Mariner's Mirror*, vol. XVIII (April 1932), pp. 168–87.

Incháustegui Cabral, Joaquín Marino. *La gran expedición inglesa contra las Antillas Mayores*. Mexico City: Gráfica Panamericana, 1953.

Rodríguez Demorizi, Emilio. *Invasión inglesa de 1655; notas adicionales de Fray Cipriano de Utrera*. Ciudad Trujillo: Montalvo, 1957.

— 'Invasión inglesa en 1655', in *Boletín del Archivo General de la Nación* (Dominican Republic), vol. 20, No. 92 (January–March 1957), pp. 6–70.

Taylor, S. A. G. *The Western Design: An Account of Cromwell's Expedition to the Caribbean*. London: Solstice Productions, 1969.

Thornton, A. P. *West-Indian Policy under the Restoration*. Oxford, 1956.

Wright, Irene Aloha. *Spanish Narratives of the English Attack on Santo Domingo, 1655*. London: Royal Historical Society, 1926.

Details of the illicit logwood trade appear in:

Gerhard, Peter. *The Southeast Frontier of New Spain*. Princeton, New Jersey: Princeton University Press, 1979.

Marcus, Linda C. 'English Influence on Belize and the Petén Region of Northern Guatemala, 1630 to 1763.' Unpublished Ph.D. thesis, Southern Methodist University, 1990.

McJunkin, David M. 'Logwood: An Inquiry into the Historical Biogeography of *Haematoxylum campechanium L.* and Related Dyewoods of the Neotropics.' Unpublished Ph.D. thesis, University of California at Los Angeles, 1991.

The careers of the famous buccaneer 'admiral' Henry Morgan and his peers are summarised in:

Cruikshank, E. A. *The Life of Sir Henry Morgan*. Toronto: Macmillan, 1935.

Earle, Peter. *The Sack of Panamá: Sir Henry Morgan's Adventures on the Spanish Main*. New York: Viking, 1981.

Hamshere, C. E. 'Henry Morgan and the Buccaneers', in *History Today*, vol. XVI (1966), pp. 406–14.

Pope, Dudley. *Harry Morgan's Way: The Biography of Sir Henry Morgan, 1635–1684*. London: Secker & Warburg, 1977.

Thornton, A. P. 'The Modyfords and Morgan', in *Jamaican Historical Review*, vol. 2 (1952), pp. 36–60.

Descriptions of seventeenth-century privateering and piratical warfare in the West Indies are contained in:

Marley, David F. *Sack of Veracruz: The Great Pirate Raid of 1683*. Windsor, Ontario, Canada: Netherlandic Press, 1993.

Pawson, Michael, and Buisseret, David J. *Port Royal, Jamaica*. Oxford: Clarendon Press, 1975.

— 'A Pirate at Port Royal in 1679', in *The Mariner's Mirror*, vol. LVII (1971), pp. 303–5.

Rubio Mañé, José Ignacio. 'Las jurisdicciones de Yucatán: la creación de la plaza de teniente de Rey en Campeche, año de 1744', in *Boletín del Archivo General de la Nación* [Mexico], Segunda Serie, vol. VII, No. 3 (July–September 1966), pp. 549–631.

Serrano Mangas, Fernando. *Los galeones de la carrera de Indias, 1650–1700*. Seville: Escuela de Estudios Hispano–americanos, 1985.

Shomette, Donald G., and Haslach, Robert D. *Raid on America: The Dutch Naval Campaign of 1672–1674*. Columbia: University of South Carolina Press, 1988.

Webster, John Clarence. *Cornelis Steenwyck: Dutch Governor of Acadie*. Ottawa: Canadian Historical Association, 1929.

Weddle, Robert S. *Wilderness Manhunt: The Spanish Search for La Salle*. Austin: University of Texas Press, 1973.

— *Spanish Sea: The Gulf of Mexico in North American Discovery, 1500–1685*. College Station: Texas A&M University Press, 1985.

Zahedieh, Nuala. 'The Merchants of Port Royal, Jamaica, and the Spanish Contraband Trade, 1655–1692', in *William and Mary Quarterly*, vol. 43, No. 4 (October 1986), pp. 570–93.

Buccaneer incursions into the Pacific Ocean are described in:

Bernal Ruiz, María del Pilar. *La toma del puerto de Guayaquil en 1687*. Seville: Escuela de Estudios Hispano–americanos, 1979.

Bradley, Peter T. *The Lure of Peru: Maritime Intrusion into the South Sea, 1598–1701*. New York: St Martin's Press, 1990.

— *Society, Economy and Defence in Seventeenth Century Peru: The Administration of the Conde de Alba de Liste (1655–61)*. Liverpool: 1992.

— 'The Ships of the Viceroyalty of Peru in the Seventeenth Century', in *The Mariner's Mirror*, vol. 79, No. 4 (November 1993), pp. 393–402.

Dyer, Florence E. 'Captain John Strong, Privateer and Treasure Hunter', in *The Mariner's Mirror*, vol. XIII (1927), pp. 145–58.

Kemp, Peter K., and Lloyd, Christopher. *The Brethren of the Coast: The British and French Buccaneers in the South Seas*. London: Heinemann, 1960.

Pérez Mallaína Bueno, Pablo Emilio, and Torres Ramírez, Bibiano. *La Armada del Mar del Sur*. Seville: Escuela de Estudios Hispano–americanos, 1987.

Serrano Mangas, Fernando. 'El proceso del pirata Bartholomew Sharp, 1682', in Seville: *Temas americanistas*, No. 4 (1984), pp. 14–18.

Incidents during the War of the League of Augsburg, which marked an end to seventeenth-century piratical activities, are described in:

Baer, Joel H. '"Captain John Avery" and the Anatomy of a Mutiny', in *Eighteenth-Century Life*, vol. 18 (February 1994), pp. 1–23.

Baudrit, André. *Charles de Courbon, Comte de Blénac, 1622–1696; Gouverneur Général des Antilles Françaises, 1677–1696*. Fort de France: Annales des Antilles, Société d'Histoire de la Martinique, 1967.

Bodge, Rev George M. 'The Dutch Pirates in Boston, 1694–5', in *Bostonian Society Publications*, vol. VII (1910), pp. 31–60.

De la Matta Rodríguez, Enrique. *El asalto de Pointis a Cartagena de Indias*. Seville: Escuela de Estudios Hispano-americanos, 1979.

López Cantos, Angel. *Historia de Puerto Rico (1650–1700)*. Seville: Escuela de Estudios Hispano-americanos, 1975.

Ritchie, Robert C. *Captain Kidd and the War Against the Pirates*. Cambridge, Massachusetts: Harvard University Press, 1986.

Rodríguez Demorizi, Emilio. 'Acerca del tratado de Ryswick', in Ciudad Trujillo, Dominican Republic: *Clio*, vol. 22, No. 100 (July–September 1954), pp. 127–32.

Sigüenza y Góngora, Carlos de. *Trofeo de la justicia española en el castigo de la alevosía francesa*. Repr. in *Obras históricas* (Mexico City: Porrúa, 1960).

— *Relación de lo sucedido a la Armada de Barlovento*. Repr. in *Obras históricas* (Mexico City: Porrúa, 1960).

Tribout de Morembert, Henri. 'A Saint-Domingue, Le Major Bernanos, capitaine de flibustiers', in Paris:

Connaissance du Monde, vol. 78 (1965), pp. 10–19.

Early eighteenth-century histories of piracy include:

Carlova, John. *Mistress of the Seas*. London: Jarrolds, 1965.

Defoe, Daniel. *The Life, Adventures and Piracies of the Famous Captain Singleton*. London: Everyman, 1963.

Driscoll, Charles B. 'Finale of the Wedding March', in *American Mercury* (July 1928), pp. 355–63.

Dupont, Étienne. *L'Aumônier des corsaires: l'Abbé Jouin (1672–1720)*. Nantes: Libraire L. Durance, 1926.

Johnson, Captain Charles. *Lives of the Most Notorious Pirates* (ed. with an introduction by Christopher Lloyd.) London: Folio Society, 1962.

Le Blant, Robert. 'Un Officier Béarnais à Saint-Domingue: Pierre-Gédéon Ier de Nolivos, Chevalier de l'Ordre Royal et Militaire de Saint-Louis, Lieutenant du Roy, puis Major du Petit Goâve et commandant de la partie Ouest de Saint-Domingue, 1706–1732.' Extrait de la *Revue Historique & Archéologique du Béarn et du Pays Basque*. Pau: Lescher– Moutoué, 1931.

Le Cozannet, Yvon, and Ducable, Gérard, eds. *Jean Doublet: le corsaire du Roi Soleil*. Monaco: Le Rocher, 1990.

Richards, Stanley. *Black Bart*. Llandybie, Carms.: Christopher Davies, 1966.

It should be noted that Peter N. Furbank and W. R. Owens's book *The Canonisation of Daniel Defoe* (New Haven: Yale University Press, 1988), has cast considerable doubt on the possibility that Defoe wrote Captain Charles Johnson's book under a pseudonym.

D. General Background
Additional information on the entire maritime world during the Golden Age of piracy can also be found in:

Craton, Michael. *A History of the Bahamas*. London: Collins, 1968.

Crouse, Nellis M. *The French Struggle for the West Indies, 1665–1713*. New York: Octagon, 1966.

Crump, Dr Helen J. *Colonial Admiralty Jurisdiction in the Seventeenth Century*. London: Longmans Green, 1931.

De Ville, Winston. *Saint Domingue: Census Records and Military Lists (1688–1720)*. Ville Platte, Louisiana: Pub. by author, 1988.

Dunn, Richard S. 'The Barbados Census of 1680: Profile of the Richest Colony in English America', in *William and Mary Quarterly*, Third Series, vol. 26 (1969), pp. 3–30.

Earle, Peter. *The Treasure of the* Concepción: *The Wreck of the* Almiranta. New York: Viking, 1980.

García Fuentes, Lutgardo. *El comercio español con América (1650–1700)*. Seville: Escuela de Estudios Hispano–americanos, 1980.

Gehring, Charles T., and Schiltkamp, Jacob A., trans. and eds. *Curaçao Papers, 1640–1665*. Vol. XVII, 'New Netherland Documents.' Interlaken, New York: Heart of the Lakes Publishing, 1987.

Gemelli Careri, Giovanni Francesco. *Viaje a la Nueva España*. Mexico City: Universidad Nacional Autónoma de México, 1976.

Goddet-Langlois, Jean and Denise. *La vie en Guadeloupe au XVIIe siècle, suivi du Dictionnaire des familles guadeloupéennes de 1635 à 1700*. Fort-de-France: Editions Exbrayat, 1991.

Goslinga, Cornelis Ch. *The Dutch in the Caribbean and on the Wild Coast, 1580–1680*. Gainesville: University of Florida Press, 1971.

— *The Dutch in the Caribbean and in the Guianas, 1680–1791*. Dover, New Hampshire: Van Gorcum, 1985.

Prebble, John. *The Darien Disaster*. London: Secker & Warburg, 1968.

Sucre, Luis Alberto. *Gobernadores y capitanes generales de Venezuela*. Caracas: Litografía Tecnocolor, 1964.

Taillemite, Etienne. *Dictionnaire des Marins Français*. Paris: Editions Maritimes et d'Outre-Mer, 1982.

Index